The 50/50

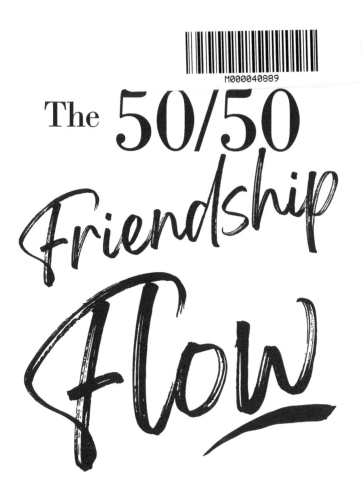

Friendship

Flow

Life Lessons From And For My Girlfriends

Shari Leid

The 50/50 Friendship Flow

Life Lessons From And For My Girlfriends

Neither the publisher nor the author is engaged in rendering professional advice or services to the individual reader. The ideas and suggestions contained in this book are not intended as a substitute for professional help. Neither the author nor the publisher shall be liable or responsible for any loss or damage allegedly arising from any information or suggestion in this book.

The views and opinions expressed in this book are the author's own and the facts are as reported by the author. They have been verified to the extent possible, and the publisher is not in any way liable for the same.

 Published by: Capucia, LLC
211 Pauline Drive #513
York, PA 17402

ISBN: 978-1-9452528-53
Library of Congress Control Number: 2020912583

Cover Design: Zizi Iryaspraha Subiyarta/www.pagatana.com
Layout: Ranilo Cabo
Cover photo: Nikki Closser/www.nikkiclosser.com
Inside photos/black and whites: Natalie Wallace/www.nataliewallacephotography.com
Editor and Proofreader: Janis Hunt Johnson/www.askjanis.com
Book Midwife: Carrie Jareed

Printed in the United States of America

The 50/50

Life Lessons From And
For My Girlfriends

This book is dedicated to my loving and supportive husband, daughter, and son — Rory, Alexis, and Zachary — who always love and support me unconditionally as I grow, learn, and experience this wonderful thing called *Life*.

"People grow through experience if they meet life honestly and courageously. This is how character is built."
— Eleanor Roosevelt

Contents

CONTENTS

Foreword

The 50/50 Friendship Flow is more than a book; it is a way of life. The author, Shari Leid, takes you along with her as she meets with 50 women over the course of a year for the purpose of sharing with each of them what she has learned from them, how they inspire her, and what they have brought to her life. Through this journey, Shari shows the impact and importance of relationships. Some of the women she meets with have been life-long friends of hers, others are much newer friendships. Shari believes that everyone she meets is both her teacher and her student.

I had the good fortune of being asked to participate in Shari's journey as one of the 50 women she chose. Because of my experience being the recipient of the 50/50 Friendship Flow Challenge, which is outlined in this book — and hearing the life lesson that I brought to Shari's life — I decided to embark on the 50/50 Friendship Flow Challenge myself. Through the Challenge, I have experienced the magic that happens when you take the time to meet one on one with the people in your life who have inspired you, simply taking the time to share with them what they have meant to you and what life lesson you have learned from them. As a participant, I felt both seen and appreciated for the value I bring to each friendship and to the world. It was a strikingly mindful experience that sparked feelings of pride, humility, and gratitude. It energized my soul!

I knew right away that I needed to share this life-changing experience with my friends in my own Friendship Flow Challenge. Shari encourages people to make the 50/50 Friendship Flow Challenge their own. So unlike Shari, who chose to meet with 50 women, I have chosen to meet with 20 people over the course of a year — many who are men — who have had an impact on my life.

As it turns out, I am not the only one to have taken up the Challenge. The 50/50 Friendship Flow Challenge has become a movement, continuing to have a ripple effect — reminding us of the great importance of relationships, and reinforcing the fact that we are all connected.

This book is designed for you to read a chapter each week, and to take action that week based on the life lesson shared. I know it will inspire you to join the 50/50 Friendship Flow Challenge yourself. I promise you, you'll never be the same.

Tanya Murdock Lewis
(Shari's Date 27)

Tanya Murdock Lewis is a licensed psychotherapist, and owner of Zen Counseling NW, which is a vibrant family and marriage therapy center located in Gig Harbor, Washington.

Introduction

Part of the beauty of your life's journey is the experience of the constant flow of people who come in and out of your life on a daily basis. Some people stay for a lifetime, others are here for a moment, and some may be in your life for just a chance 30-second meeting. This book is about the power of female friendships. Each woman who comes into your life is both your teacher and your student. The teachings can come in the form of an inspiration, a life lesson, or a life blessing.

It is rare to set aside time to meet one on one with individuals for the sole purpose of telling them how much they mean to you, and to let them know what a profound influence they have had in your life. *This changes now.*

The Beginning

The 50/50 Friendship Flow Challenge project began in December of 2018. I happened to be turning 49 that month, which prompted me to seriously ponder what I wanted my life to look like — not just at 50 years of age, but also what I wanted my life to be from then on.

My 40s were a time for both mental and spiritual growth, much of which stemmed from several significant physical challenges. The biggest life-changing physical challenge occurred in 2017, when I received a breast cancer diagnosis at age 47. My children were 17 and 15 at the time of my diagnosis. I will never forget the day that my husband and I called for a family meeting — something that had become quite rare as the children grew older, since they were each carving out their own lives by this time and had become increasingly independent. My 15-year-old son, who had noticed that his dad had taken my place on several recent school pick-ups, responded to the news of my diagnosis with "I knew." He could tell something was wrong. Kids are perceptive that way. My daughter asked questions and noticed my husband's eyes fill with tears as I told my children that I received a breast cancer diagnosis, but said, "I know everything is going to be okay."

Although I said everything was going to be okay, the severity of my diagnosis and the prognosis were still unknowns.

Three months following that heart-wrenching family discussion, I underwent a double mastectomy. It would prove to be a tough two years for me following the surgery. Through those two years, it became crystal clear to me that health was a gift. By becoming healthy once again, I was given the opportunity to live each day to the fullest. I began to reflect upon and recognize the vast importance of the relationships in my life.

I made it my mission not to allow another year to go by where I did not take the time to sit down one on one with each of my girlfriends to share the meaning that she brought to my life. I proceeded to make a list of 50 women who I wanted to meet with over the course of one year. Some women on the list were longtime friends, others were relatively new acquaintances.

I was intentional with whom I chose — purposeful with both the questions I asked and the dialogue that I hoped to have. I listened carefully to the words shared with me, and I spoke to each woman from my heart and soul. I let go of my own ego. I was there to be both the teacher and the student. This project of mine has become so powerful that it has evolved into not just a personal endeavor, but a movement — which you now know is called "The 50/50 Friendship Flow Challenge."

During my 50/50 Friendship Flow Challenge journey, I discovered that the gift of one-on-one time with each girlfriend — sharing with her the strength and wisdom that she has brought to my life — often brought her to tears of gratitude, learning, and a deeper human connection than I could have ever imagined. The meetings were even more powerful than I had first thought. As I posted about these meetings on my personal Facebook page — in a photo album that I entitled "50 Dates," the album became increasingly popular and followed by many.

I had thrown a pebble into the ocean, and the waves it made were far-reaching.

Take the Challenge

The 50/50 Friendship Flow Challenge can take any form you would like. I challenge you to set up at least 20 one-on-one meetings over the course of the year, because it is a significant commitment. It requires time, planning, and thought. It is not easy. It forces you to take time out of your busy life to focus on what is often neglected but which holds such huge significance — our human connections. The Challenge requires a commitment which becomes part of your life for a whole year. But if 20 seems like too many, then ten is fine. Even five lives touched is much better than none. Or be bold and try 50, as I did — or even 52, one meeting per week.

Whatever you choose in numbers, please be sure to commit fully and record your journey. You can document your journey publicly through social media, or privately through a journal. I guarantee that your life will become fuller because of this — and the ripple effect of sitting down one on one to share your feelings with another person will reap unexpected rewards.

For the people you choose to meet with, the gift you'll give them — of being seen and heard — is remarkable. When you recognize the importance of the people in your life, it will keep you living in a world filled with gratitude and grace. I chose to meet with 50 women in 50 different restaurants, but you can meet anywhere. It does not need to cost anything other than the gift of time, which has immeasurable value.

I have captured my meetings in the following pages. The stories are written in chronological order as the dates took place, not necessarily grouped by similar subjects or in any particular order of perceived importance. It is also noteworthy that I did not plan these dates in any particular order; I simply had a list of women pre-selected, and when we were able to find the time to meet, that is when we met. As the process played out, I quickly learned that there was no order that needed to be preplanned, because every life lesson, every single meeting, was just as important as the last, and the next.

What started out as a personal project, my 50 dates with 50 women, has taken on an entirely new meaning. What I found is that the 50/50 Friendship Flow Challenge is an exchange — a giving and receiving — a back-and-forth relationship. Remember: Every person you meet is both your teacher and your student.

It is said that a great book is one that you can pick up and read again and again, learning something new each time. I hope this book is that for you. Read this book slowly. Read one date per week, or no more than one per day. Focus in on the lesson of that date. The lesson will mean something different to each of us, because we all perceive life and life's lessons through our own filters, through our own history. Learn from these 50 women who are in my life, and soon you will recognize the lessons that you have learned from the people in your own life. Once you engage in this practice regularly, you will find that you will automatically focus on the blessings that each person you come across brings to your life. Write in the margins, fill the blank pages, date your notes, and use this book as a journal of your journey. Let's learn together.

Join the 50/50 Friendship Flow Challenge today!

The 50/50 Friendship Flow Challenge:

(1) Set a date. One on one.
(2) Set your intention and let go of ego.
(3) Share your admiration and your observations.
(4) Ask questions.
(5) Finally, write it down, take a photo, keep a journal, and capture the moment.

#5050friendshipflowchallenge

The 50/50 Friendship Flow Challenge

"Family and friends and faith are the most important things in your life and you should be building friendships"
—Barbara Bush

Chapter 1

Use Your Gifts and Talents

Date 1 — December 3, 2018, Monday
JOEY Bellevue, Bellevue, Washington
Happy Hour
Girlfriend: CC

My girlfriend CC moved from Seattle to Detroit, Michigan a couple of years ago, but despite her move she kept her job in Seattle. She commutes from Detroit to Seattle several times a month to tend to her job as a Program Officer for a philanthropic foundation based out of Seattle. I happened to catch her on one of her trips to Seattle. CC is a cute, round-faced Black American woman who is in her mid-40s, married to a man of Jewish descent who is just a few years her senior. She has the best smile, which she shares authentically. In other words, CC is not going to smile at you simply to be pleasant. If you receive one of her million-dollar smiles, you know it comes from the heart. She and I are close in height, with neither of us being too far above five feet tall. CC has an adult daughter who is of a beautiful Japanese, Black, and White ethnic mix and who possesses the gift of spontaneous lyrical improvisation, which has led her to the stage in a number of east-coast rap battles. CC also has two younger children, both of Black and White ethnic mixes, a high-school-aged son and a middle-school-aged daughter. While her children are of mixed race, I have witnessed the importance that both CC and her husband have placed upon actively making sure that their children understand Black American culture and their place in it.

CC and I met approximately ten years ago. At the time we met, our young sons played on the same neighborhood soccer team in South Seattle. My family had a home in the Seward Park neighborhood and CC's family had a home north of us in the Mount Baker neighborhood. While both neighborhoods, especially Mount Baker, are thought of as more affluent areas of South Seattle, the area is in general known for lower housing prices and great racial diversity. While CC and I were cordial during these soccer games, making small talk when we passed one another, we never had a conversation of any substance until we happened to be seated together at a mother-and-son event at a private Seattle club that had not allowed racial minorities to join until after the Civil Rights Movement. We found ourselves in a room filled with predominately White women — many one-percenters — historically the demographics that these types of private clubs draw. We had been seated alone by the club with our sons at a table that seated eight, in a back corner of the grand ballroom. Being seated alone turned out to be a blessing for CC and me. Our conversation flowed easily. We learned that we both grew up in the same area of Seattle (which was a more impoverished area of South Seattle), and we found that we had attended rival high schools. It was the start of a close and dear friendship, and many more dinners, parties, and valued conversations followed.

Interestingly, CC was one of the few women who, prior to our 50/50 Friendship Flow Challenge date, I had gotten together with one on one quite regularly, which was unusual for me. Typically, I chose to get together with friends in larger groups — at least that is what I did prior to my experience with the power of the 50/50 Friendship Flow Challenge. I realize now that I always enjoy getting together with CC, because I can simply be myself, a homegirl from South Seattle.

If you were to look at CC's life story, you would find an inspiring account of a woman who went from being a single teenage mom to a Yale University graduate — a woman who was the 2019 Yale University's Women's Award for Excellence recipient and who has served on Yale University's Board of Governors. It is hard not to be impressed, and even a little intimidated by her resume. Not only that, but CC is involved in her community. She sits on numerous boards and has been involved in a number of conferences and committees, many which she has organized or chaired. CC has a passion for giving back to her community and working with the less privileged to find ways to empower them to succeed, mostly through education.

When I sat down with CC, I shared with her that I am often asked to serve on boards or committees, and historically I almost always decline because I felt I was not up to par. I had a voice in my head that told me that I do not possess the background or experience to be effective. Without hesitation, CC shared with me that she knows that she is enough, and that she has something of value to share and to contribute, even on boards where the majority does not look like her. As I spoke to CC about my hesitation to get involved, she emphasized my value, my worth. She reminded me that my voice is important, and that these messages of self-doubt do not serve me. Although she did not say it directly, I felt as if she were telling me that I have been given many gifts — talents which I am foolishly wasting by not getting involved in my community — and that I have a duty to share my voice.

The 50/50 Friendship Flow Challenge Lesson: It's important to offer your gifts and your talents, because you have been given the opportunity to make a difference in your community.

The 50/50 Friendship Flow Challenge to Take Action: Notice the many opportunities that you have in front of you, which are just waiting for the contribution of your unique gifts and talents.

Journal

Today's date is:

My gifts and talents are:

Your gifts and talents have been given to you to make the world a better place. Share them freely.

Chapter 2

Practice Gratitude Daily

Date 2 — December 6, 2018, Thursday

Barking Frog, Woodinville, Washington

Lunch

Girlfriend: Elyse

My girlfriend Elyse is a striking, dark-haired, blue-eyed Greek Jewish beauty. She is slender, and appears to be of runway-model height, in part due to the fashionable high heels that she loves to wear. Elyse attended the University of Washington and graduated a few years after me. She is in her early 40s, married, and is a mom to a grade-school-aged son. After graduating from the University of Washington, she attended school in Paris, receiving a Certificate in Fashion Merchandising, Design, and Marketing. She has remained in the industry of fashion, styling, and marketing while choosing projects that have allowed her the flexibility to spend time with her son during his early childhood.

Elyse and I met in June of 2017. I was hosting a shopping-party girls' night at my home, which featured several of my girlfriends who were jewelry, clothing, and handbag designers. I have always been attracted to creative souls. Elyse was invited to the party at my home through a mutual girlfriend who recognized how close in proximity our homes are located. From the moment Elyse walked into my house, we clicked. It is hard to describe what makes certain people easier than others to connect with, but some simply are — and Elyse was one of those people to me. Over the next couple of years, we spent more and more time to together, meeting for lunch, carpooling together to events, and going on many girls' nights out. We freely introduced each other to each of our friends, which widened both our social circles.

Every time I see Elyse, one of the first words out of her mouth is how happy she is to see me. It is not something that she just says as lip service; it comes from her heart. You can tell by the warmth of her smile and the sparkle in her eyes that she is genuine in her words. And that is the way Elyse lives. She lives in gratitude. She lives grateful for the people in her life and for the experiences she has. She enters the room with an energy that is like no other I've seen, and I believe it is this spirit of living in gratitude that shines so brightly through her. She enjoys her experiences and her time with others immensely, and that joy overflows. She loves to go out and socialize with friends, and absolutely loves to entertain at her home. I often witness Elyse quickly offering her house as a meeting location for socializing either before or after an event, inviting everyone over to her beautiful home. She is a spontaneous host, focusing on the moments with others rather than worrying about what her home should look like or if she has enough food and drink for everyone. There is of course always plenty, and her home is continuously filled with candles, flowers, and warmth.

During our 50/50 Friendship Flow Challenge date, I shared with Elyse that I want more of the energy that she brings wherever she goes. I want to walk into a room and lift the vibration of the room to a higher level, as she so effortlessly does. I believe that her particular magic comes from living in gratitude. It is perceptibly felt by others.

Immediately following our lunch date, I began to post about our date in my Facebook 50 Dates Album, and while posting, a text came in from Elyse that read, "I'm so grateful for our time together today."

My 50/50 Friendship Flow Challenge lesson from Elyse is not only to live in gratitude but also to tell the people in your life how much you appreciate them. I am glad she was my number-two date in this process because it just reinforces the overall message of this project. Live in gratitude, and tell the people in your life that you are grateful for them.

The 50/50 Friendship Flow Challenge Lesson: Living each day with gratitude is a way of life, not a duty.

The 50/50 Friendship Flow Challenge to Take Action: When you wake up each morning, take a moment to set an intention to live the day in gratitude.

Journal

Today's date is:

_____

Today I am grateful for:

_____

_____

_____

_____

_____

_____

_____

_____

_____

_____

_____

_____

_____

_____

Living in gratitude is where the soul shines.

Chapter 3

Focus on the Strengths of Those You Lead

Date 3 — December 6, 2018, Thursday
Etta's and Queen City, Seattle, Washington
Happy Hour
Girlfriend: Kayley

tta's is a wonderful northwest eatery which is located near the iconic Pike Place Market, while Queen City is located in the trendy Belltown neighborhood of Seattle. Its website lists the establishment as "Seattle's oldest bar, maybe." Kayley and I had such a great evening together, we managed to fit in two stops during our 50/50 Friendship Flow Challenge date.

Kayley is a blue-eyed blonde, relatively tall, and physically fit. Like me, she has lived her entire life in Seattle. She is in her late

40s, a stepmom to three adult children, and a mom to a high-school-aged daughter and a high-school-aged son. She holds a Bachelor of Arts and a Master's in Teaching, and has enjoyed a long career in teaching, currently working as a Learning Specialist at a Seattle-area private school, where she specializes in teaching children with dyslexia and other learning differences. She was just a year behind me in high school, having attended and graduated from one of the area's most prestigious private high schools. Kayley is a Seattleite through and through. Kayley comes from an established Seattle family where values of local philanthropy, education, and service to the community were instilled as a young child. She has followed in her family's footsteps, with a passion for community involvement, as she actively serves on a number of non-profit boards and committees throughout the Seattle area. As I describe Kayley's family history, I realize that it was actually years after I met her that I discovered her family's prominence in our city. For the longest time, I simply knew her as my friend, Kayley.

Kayley and I met through a mutual friend, approximately ten years ago, at a girls' night out. Actually, we probably called it a "moms' night out" back then, since our kids were all in grade school — the age where many women view themselves first and foremost as moms, and it seems everything is associated with that title. While we had fun together that first night with our girlfriends, we truly became friends later that year when Kayley signed up for a mixed martial arts fitness class that I was teaching.

When Kayley sat down with me for our 50/50 Friendship Flow Challenge date, I immediately told her that I wanted to discuss her gift of leadership. I have witnessed Kayley's ability to lead in a number of situations. It comes so naturally to her that I sometimes doubt that she fully recognizes her power. She has the skill to quickly assess a situation and respond accordingly in a way that brings people together. It is her gift. She looks for the win for everyone, without losing sight of the goal.

I appreciate how incredibly inclusive Kayley is. As I mentioned above, it was years before I understood the prominence of Kayley's family in Seattle. Kayley, while proud of her family, never uses her family's position to take unfair advantage of another person. I have attended events with Kayley where I have witnessed people reacting to her family name and its prominence in our city, and then I watch them quickly assume things about Kayley's character before getting to know her. In every instance, I have only seen her respond with a gracious smile and then proceed to try to get to know the other person. What matters most to Kayley is the true nature of a person, and how that person treats others, not a person's financial or social status; and she hopes that other people will ultimately treat her the same way.

From my observations of Kayley, I perceive her strength in being a gentle leader. She leads by focusing on and understanding others. She believes that everyone can contribute and make a difference. She gives everyone she leads the opportunity and the support that they need to succeed. Kayley focuses on the strengths of those whom she leads — not on their weaknesses.

The 50/50 Friendship Flow Challenge Lesson: To be an effective leader, bring out the strengths of those whom you lead, instead of focusing on yourself and what boosts your own ego.

The 50/50 Friendship Flow Challenge to Take Action: Focus on the strengths of those whom you lead rather than on their weaknesses, and set out to watch their strengths quickly grow, while their weaknesses diminish.

Journal

Today's date is:

_____

I recognize and support the strengths of those whom I lead, at home and at work, in the following ways:

_____

_____

_____

_____

_____

_____

_____

_____

_____

_____

_____

_____

_____

Great leaders focus on the strengths, not on the weaknesses, of the individuals they lead.

Chapter 4

Simply Smile

Date 4 — December 11, 2018, Tuesday
BluWater Bistro, Leschi, Seattle, Washington
Dinner
Girlfriend: Dede

Dede is a tall Black American woman with beautiful, rich dark skin. She wears her hair in a short, smart, stylish cut, and her glasses frame her face perfectly. Dede has a vibrant career, holding a Master's in Social Work, and in recent years she has held the position of Dean of Student Life at an independent Seattle-area girls' middle school. Her most prominent feature is her big, beautiful smile.

Dede and I met at a mutual friend's birthday party approximately five years ago. Following the first evening we met, we found ourselves together at several other social events, and our relationship naturally blossomed over time. Dede brings an energy to a room that makes everyone around her feel welcome. It is not surprising that I, like many others, was immediately drawn to her.

It can easily be said that Dede "meets more strangers than any of us." However, this is not entirely true. We all meet the same number of strangers — people we do not know. The difference is that Dede truly *meets* strangers. She believes that everyone has the ability to thrive and survive, and that everyone has a story to tell.

When Dede shared her philosophy with me, I could not help but immediately think of how fortunate the girls are at the school where she is Dean of Student Life, to have someone in her position who believes in every one of her students. I actually get emotional when I think of girls at such a vulnerable age — those tricky middle-school years — having an outstanding female role model like Dede.

Dede has a smile that draws people to her, and she cannot help but smile. Most recently, she posted a story on her personal Facebook page about an experience she had while waiting at one of Seattle's over 100 Starbucks stores. She noticed that a man was staring at her from across the room. While many of us would immediately become defensive when seeing a man looking at us from across a room, perhaps even roll our eyes at him to discourage his interest, Dede instead acknowledged him. She smiled at him and truly saw him as an individual. Long story short, he took a seat next to her and she listened to him. She fully listened to him. She learned that he was a former Army Ranger who had fallen on hard times and he was now homeless. He explained to her that she reminded him of his former wife, which is what initially caught his eye. She listened to his whole story. He was not dressed in the finest threads nor did he have the best hygiene. She noticed his missing teeth and his disheveled appearance, but she saw past his physical appearance and recognized his humanity.

Until my 50/50 Friendship Flow Challenge date with Dede, I fully believed that I also saw people. In fact, the simple act of doing the 50/50 Friendship Flow Challenge is a way to learn how to really see someone. What I found out from meeting up with Dede is that I do not always see everyone. I realized that I have often chosen not to see the homeless vet at Starbucks, I have chosen not to see the timid girl no one believes in, and I have chosen not to see those who do not agree with me. In the past, I really have not seen the people Dede sees. But this changes now. I am going to share my smile the way Dede does so effortlessly.

The 50/50 Friendship Flow Challenge Lesson: Don't underestimate the power of a smile to brighten someone's day.

The 50/50 Friendship Flow Challenge to Take Action: Practice truly seeing people today. Share your smile.

Journal

Today's date is:

_____

I've noticed that when I smile, the response I receive from people around me brightens the world in the following ways:

_____

_____

_____

_____

_____

_____

_____

_____

_____

_____

_____

_____

_____

_____

It costs nothing to smile. And it can actually make a difference in someone else's life.

"Being able to recognize what
makes you happy, is the first
step to a life filled
with happiness."
—Shari Leid

Chapter 5

Live Your Values

Date 5 — December 15, 2018, Saturday
Meet the Moon, Seattle, Washington
Brunch
Girlfriend: Martha

I met Martha approximately 13 years ago when our oldest daughters were students in the same kindergarten class. We met during the summer prior to the start of school at one of those awkward new family meet-and-greets. Although our daughters attended school together for what amounted to less than three school years, Martha and I remained friends. Over the past several years, we have made it a point to get together regularly, sometimes for coffee, often for wine.

Martha and I happen to be about the same physical size and age. She wears the trendiest eyeglasses, and would proudly tell you that she is a self-described nerd. She is an intellect, a writer, a teacher, a mom to two high-school-aged girls, and a wife to a man whom I suspect she would easily describe as her best friend. Martha graduated with a Bachelor of Arts degree in Classics and English from Stanford University. She grew up in a family where education was highly valued, and gifts of intellect run deep.

Not too long ago, I had the privilege of attending a book launch at the University of Washington Bookstore for Martha's most recent book, *Unpresidented*, which is a biography of Donald Trump. I learned so much that evening — not simply historical facts about President Trump, but about what real moral fiber actually is. Martha relayed a personal story: She shared that when as a young girl she read *The Diary of Anne Frank*, it had a profound effect on her. As a child, she wondered what type of person she would be had she lived in Anne Frank's time and place. Martha wondered whether she would have been a Nazi or if she would have been a protector of the Jewish people. And she shared that she recalled, even as a child, wanting to believe that she would have been a protector, someone who stands up for those who are oppressed. This is the person that Martha has strived to be all of her life — a person of integrity who would be a protector for those who do not have the ability to protect themselves.

During this same author presentation, Martha stated, "What you do, when you have power, represents your true character." I found the statement so profound that I pulled out my iPhone to take down her quote while I was seated in the audience.

When we met for brunch for our 50/50 Friendship Flow Challenge date, I shared with Martha that I wanted to understand why she continues to speak up, when in my view, she could often get by much more easily by remaining quiet. I look at her and I see someone who came from a well-educated and financially secure family — a White woman, who attended the same elite private school as Bill Gates, and who graduated from Stanford. I see someone who does not need to make noise against social injustice, especially when it leads to a heavy personal burden for her, including receiving hatred from those who oppose her views. Martha explained that she cannot stay quiet because racism, sexism, classism, and discrimination of any sort eat at her core.

I have so much appreciation for Martha. She is one of my biggest role models. She reminds me of the importance of aligning my actions with my values, even when inaction may be an easier road. Martha expresses her gifts as a writer and presenter; she is someone who is able to get her message of simple humanity across in a compassionate way without being threatening. She embraces her gifts, and through that she is making a positive difference in the world.

The 50/50 Friendship Flow Challenge Lesson: While actions may often speak louder than words, inaction also speaks just as loudly.

The 50/50 Friendship Flow Challenge to Take Action: Decide today to live your values.

Journal

Today's date is:

_____

Here is how I will live my values:

_____

_____

_____

_____

_____

_____

_____

_____

_____

_____

_____

_____

While actions speak louder than words, inaction speaks just as loudly. There is always something you can do to make a difference.

"My goal is to take every conflict, every experience, and learn from it."

—Shari Leid

Chapter 6

Show Your Strength
with Kindness

Date 6 — December 19, 2018, Wednesday
Targy's Tavern, Seattle, Washington
Late Happy Hour at a dive bar
Girlfriend: Vanessa

Vanessa and I met approximately 15 years ago at a Seattle-area mixed martial arts studio. Although Vanessa had been at the school much longer than I had, she never treated me like a newbie. She welcomed me immediately. If you are familiar with martial arts, in some schools it can feel like the military — in the sense that you need to do the time to earn the respect of the more experienced senior members. Vanessa never made me feel as if I were of lesser ability than she was, even though I clearly was behind her in experience and physical ability. She never hesitated to partner with me in drills during class and even offered to practice between classes to help me develop my skills. From the first day I met Vanessa, she showed me kindness. Her welcoming spirit was not just something only I experienced; it is how she interacts with everyone she meets. If you were to ask someone to describe Vanessa, I guarantee that the word *kind* would be included in the description.

During our 50/50 Friendship Flow Challenge date, I mentioned to Vanessa that people often confuse kindness for weakness, when in fact kindness is such an incredible strength. While I was sharing this with her, she smiled knowingly and told me that she has a quote in her car that reads, "Do not mistake kindness for weakness."

Vanessa reminds me that the best way I can show my confidence and strength each day is to act in the spirit of kindness.

The 50/50 Friendship Flow Challenge Lesson: Living in kindness shows your strength and confidence far more than living in judgment ever will.

The 50/50 Friendship Flow Challenge to Take Action: In moments of conflict, you'll find your power when you come from a place of kindness rather than with a hostile heart.

Journal

Today's date is:

_____

I am most powerful when I choose kindness rather than spitefulness.
For example:

_____

_____

_____

_____

_____

_____

_____

_____

_____

_____

_____

_____

_____

The power of kindness trumps fear, hate, hostility, and anger.

Chapter 7

Be Unforgettable

Date 7 — December 20, 2018, Thursday
Nordstrom Habitant, Bellevue, Washington
Happy Hour
Girlfriend: Lizzy

Lizzy is fiercely independent. She has the cutest laugh and simply exudes joy. She has earned a black belt in mixed martial arts, she has bow-hunted wild turkey, and she could drink most men under the table. She plays a mean game of golf, she has jumped out of an airplane, and she's trekked up mountainsides. Lizzy lives life to the fullest, never passing up an opportunity to experience a new adventure. She and I met about 20 years ago when we were both employed by the same insurance company. I was one of the company's litigation attorneys, providing defense in civil lawsuits — defending either the insurance company or the company's insureds — while Lizzy was employed as a claims adjuster, working on many of the company's higher-end litigation files. She and I were assigned to the same case. I do not recall the details of the case, but I do remember that it was an uninsured motorist claim that headed to arbitration. Lizzy and I worked together for several months, communicating through phone calls and emails. This was well before the time of video conferencing or social media. When we arrived at the arbitration, we were both surprised to discover that the other was also Asian. We did not mention it at the time of our meeting, but as we became friends over the years, we have looked back and laughed at that moment. If only there had been cartoon speech bubbles floating over our heads at that instant when we met in person.

Even if I had met Lizzy just that one time, I would not have forgotten her. She is unforgettable. Lizzy makes friends easily, and she holds onto them for a lifetime. I hoped that our 50/50 Friendship Flow Challenge date would uncover her singular magic. As we laughed and talked over lunch, I realized that Lizzy approaches new acquaintances as if they are already her friends. Her welcoming approach puts people at ease and they often immediately respond in kind. Every time I have seen a photo with Lizzy and another person — whether it be a new work relationship or a social relationship — the person she is pictured with is smiling from ear to ear. There is a genuine happiness that Lizzy brings out in everyone she meets.

Lizzy is still the girl I met 20 years ago. She is the one who meets you on the phone and does not care at all about what you look like, what kind of car you drive, or where you live. She only cares about who you are as a person. She's so welcoming, she talks to you as if she already knows you. Then, when she meets you in person, I imagine Lizzy thinking to herself, "Wow, that wasn't the picture in my mind that I had of her, but oh my goodness, it's so great to finally meet her in the flesh."

Lizzy does not simply meet people; she meets friends. Her loyalty is part of what makes her unforgettable.

The 50/50 Friendship Flow Challenge Lesson: Beginning a relationship as if you are already friends not only provides the basis for a long-lasting relationship; it makes you unforgettable.

The 50/50 Friendship Flow Challenge to Take Action: Greet new people who come into your life as you would an old friend.

Journal

Today's date is:

I can greet everyone I meet with a warmth of friendship that is unforgettable.
Here's how:

Every person you meet could end up being a friend.

"Envy can destroy a beautiful
life; it can never build one."
—Shari Leid

Chapter 8

Turn Your Problems into Opportunities

Date 8 — January 5, 2019, Saturday
Café Cesura, Bellevue, Washington
Coffee
Girlfriend: Jen

Jen and I met approximately ten years ago at a ladies' brunch. We were all seated in a restaurant at a long rectangular table. It was one of those restaurant tables that makes it difficult to talk to anyone unless they're seated directly across, or just to the left or right. Because of the seating arrangement, Jen and I did not have the opportunity to interact much during the brunch. However, thanks to social media, Jen and I kept in touch. We truly bonded when we learned that both of our daughters were having challenges in school — which only moms and dads of children who struggle in a traditional educational environment could understand.

Jen has been my rock on many occasions over the past decade, especially at those moments when I felt like a complete failure as a parent. Even though her daughter's educational challenges far outweighed mine, she never made me feel as if my concerns and emotions were unimportant. From the day I met her, Jen has been a person whom I can text, "I'm having a crappy day," and she could simply reply, "I hear you," and I know that she really has heard me. I know that she is not blowing me off with a simple response, but that she actually acknowledges me. Jen's simple words are often all that I need.

I met with Jen for the 50/50 Friendship Flow Challenge because I am fascinated by her ability to take any problems that are presented to her and quickly turn those problems into opportunities. She always takes a negative and finds the positive. She does this naturally, both professionally and personally. I am blessed not only to have a friend whom I can freely contact on my challenging days as well as on my carefree days; I am blessed to have a friend who reminds me that within each problem, an opportunity exists.

The 50/50 Friendship Flow Challenge Lesson: Inside every problem there is an opportunity for a solution.

The 50/50 Friendship Flow Challenge to Take Action: Find the opportunity that exists inside a problem you've been having.

Journal

Today's date is:

I stepped away from my emotions around the following problem, which allowed me to clearly see the opportunity that's right in front of me.

The Universe presents us with problems in order to provide us with opportunities for growth and change.

Chapter 9

Recognize Your Unique Value

Date 9 — January 6, 2019, Sunday
The Hart and The Hunter, Seattle, Washington
Dinner
Girlfriend: Diane

Diane and I met just a year ago. Despite being able to count on one hand the number of times we have gotten together, it was important for me to include her as part of my 50/50 Friendship Flow Challenge journey. Upon meeting Diane, I was immediately struck by her self-confidence. She knows who she is, she knows her value in the world — and it shows. Diane models what we can accomplish when we recognize, accept, and move through the world knowing our unique importance in our communities.

Her awareness of her own unique value has allowed Diane to transition from a successful career in social work to becoming an entrepreneur in the tech industry — an industry historically dominated by men. As Diane's business has grown, her passion for advocating for and empowering women has never wavered. She is an effective mentor to women because she knows her value and therefore abandons ego, which is often a block to success in every industry.

Being able to recognize my own value is something that, at nearly 50 years of age, I am finally achieving. Throughout so much of my childhood and young adult life, I based my value on external objectives, which lead me to nothing but insecurity and disappointment.

During our 50/50 Friendship Flow Challenge date, Diane reinforced for me the point that my value comes from within. She reminds me that knowing my value comes from a place of living authentically, recognizing and accepting my missteps without judgment, and remembering that I have unique gifts to share, from which my community can benefit.

The 50/50 Friendship Flow Challenge Lesson: You have unique value, which the world needs.

The 50/50 Friendship Flow Challenge to Take Action: Write down a list of at least ten words that describe your distinctive value.

Journal

Today's date is:

_____

The ten qualities (or more) that come to mind, which describe my exceptional value are:

_____

_____

_____

_____

_____

_____

_____

_____

_____

_____

_____

_____

_____

_____

I know who I am: I have unique, remarkable value to contribute to this world.

Chapter 10

Get Rid of the B.S.

Date 10 — January 10, 2019, Thursday
Daniel's Broiler, South Lake Union, Seattle, Washington
Happy Hour
Girlfriend: Tori

Tori is an attractive, thinly built woman in her early 50s who can easily be described as a self-made woman. She does not apologize for spending money on herself, because it is money that she alone has made. She even purchased a home on her own at a very young age in one of the most sought-after neighborhoods in Seattle. After graduating from The Foster School of Business at the University of Washington, Tori began a solo accounting practice that specializes in keeping the books for boutique law firms in the Seattle area. In addition to her accounting career, she has also flipped a house or two — simply as a hobby. I would be remiss if I did not also mention Tori's dog, Rocco, whom she adores and who has been her dear companion for over ten years.

Tori and I met through a mutual friend about eight years ago, an attorney whom she worked for at the time. We met at a girls' night out dinner and instantly hit it off. From the first day I met her, I realized that with Tori, there is simply no room for bullsh*t. To live with no B.S. means to live authentically. It is not to be brash nor overly opinionated — because Tori is neither of those things. She holds others to the same standards she holds for herself: Be honest, kind, sincere, and reliable.

I asked Tori to be one of my 50/50 Friendship Flow Challenge dates because I really appreciate and admire her integrity. She never compromises her truth to give a false opinion because it happens to be popular, nor does she compromise her truth to gain admirers. She is not overbearing with her opinions but will always be honest when asked. She will not try to color the truth or make situations appear worse than they are. I have heard Tori admit when she is wrong and I have heard her say with conviction that she is right — which, more often than not, she is!

I am thankful to have Tori in my life. She reminds me that it is more important to speak my truth even if it may not make everyone feel great, rather than to be dishonest in order to spare feelings or to try to gain acceptance. She reminds me that one of the cornerstones for any authentic relationship is truth. I love the fact that Tori models what it is to have relationships without B.S. And I cherish my friendships which have no B.S. attached.

The 50/50 Friendship Flow Challenge Lesson: There is no room for B.S. in authentic relationships.

The 50/50 Friendship Flow Challenge to Take Action: Either change or release any of your relationships that are riddled with a bunch of B.S.

Journal

Today's date is:

_____

These are the relationships in my life that lift me up because they contain no B.S.:

_____

_____

_____

_____

_____

_____

_____

_____

_____

_____

_____

_____

_____

_____

Relationships that allow you to live your truth are the relationships that bring you wellbeing.

"A roadblock is life's sign,
telling you that it is time for
you to take a detour."
—Shari Leid

50/50 FRIENDSHIP FLOW CHALLENGE

TESTIMONIAL

Kristen Jawad, Owner, Women's Wellness Education
Kirkland, Washington

When possible, I meet with the women I have chosen to connect with by going for a walk together. Essentially, the movement of walking stimulates a perfect human pace and helps us focus on each other. The fresh air draws out hopes and provides a path to finding our own footing. Trusting that the ground will meet our feet, and under our own power, we can become fully present to ourselves and for each other.

What I've learned so far:
1. Deep human connection cannot move faster than the rate at which trust can grow.
2. When we walk, we find the space to ask questions and explore the answers.
3. On these walk-and-talks, time slows down, so we can reconnect with our true desires and our creativity.
4. Ultimately, women function best when they interact with their communities, when they know they matter, and when they are invited to express themselves by making their own pathways.
5. You can shift your mood and direct your energy by simply going for a walk.
6. In our dark moments, even small steps make life better.

I am blessed to live a few minutes away from a 326-acre state park with foot paths, a quiet grotto and 3,000 feet of shoreline on Lake Washington. I have loved my one-on-one connection dates so much that I decided to create a walking group called Women in the Woods on Wednesdays, and this park is where we meet. Nature is a sanctuary for me. As a Highly Sensitive Person, I have never really felt comfortable in a commercial gym setting. It's lovely to witness the intimate conversations of the women who pair up. The fresh air and moving meditation are exceedingly restorative for my soul. I'm grateful that this idea resonates with others!

Chapter 11

Be an Active Listener

Date 11 — February 7, 2019, Thursday
Mama Melina Ristorante and Pizzeria, Seattle, Washington
Dinner
Girlfriend: Barb

I met Barb approximately 12 years ago. She is in her 60s, with blonde hair and bright blue eyes, with a slender athletic build. Barb is often mistaken for someone 20 years younger than her chronological years. Barb was my wonderful hairstylist, a hair extension specialist for several years when she was employed at a local hair salon. She and I hit it off from the moment we met. Because hair extension appointments are hours long, Barb and I had the opportunity at each visit to spend a lot of time with one another and to get deep into conversation. We discussed everything — from our kids, to relationships, to friendships, to careers, to the afterlife, and to all sorts of philosophical and social issues. I always look forward to my time with Barb because she does not blindly listen to my words, she actively listens. She has the unique ability to fully listen while analyzing what she hears. She has the ability to bring a conversation to a higher level.

Speaking with Barb is similar to being dropped into a think tank where brainstorming is encouraged. Barb's own words highlight the importance of active listening and how it works: "When a conflict occurs, I've learned to not focus on and immediately react to someone's action. I listen, and I take a moment to realize what the intent is, or the driving force behind the action; then I respond to that."

Barb reminds me to not be lazy with my conversations with friends. She has taught me to actively listen — and take a beat to analyze, offering room for ideas and solutions to flow.

The 50/50 Friendship Flow Challenge Lesson: Active listening makes for better conversations.

The 50/50 Friendship Flow Challenge to Take Action: Provide a space for brainstorming. Active listening can elevate any conversation.

Journal

Todays date is:

_____

These are the questions I will ask my friends in order to elevate our conversations:

_____

_____

_____

_____

_____

_____

_____

_____

_____

_____

_____

_____

_____

Brainstorming can be the start of something great.

Chapter 12

Find Your Power through Quiet Leadership

Date 12 — February 25, 2019, Monday
Park Lane Public House, Kirkland, Washington
Lunch
Girlfriend: Michelle

Michelle and I met a little over a decade ago. She is of Japanese German descent, in her late 40s, with hazel eyes and long black hair. When I think of Michelle's gift to the world, I think of a quiet leader.

As children in a classroom, we became conditioned to believe that the leaders are the students who speak the loudest and most often, because they are the ones who are frequently rewarded by the teacher, regularly taking over projects and conversations. If we aren't careful, we will believe that this is what a leader should look and sound like. Yet being loud and demanding does not make for effective leadership. Michelle reminds me of the inner and moral characteristics that embody a strong leader.

While I have chosen the word *quiet* to describe Michelle, I am not referring to timidity. Quite the opposite. There is power in the calm of quietude. Vice-President of a hospital at the age of 27, and now working as the Executive Director of a Washington State non-profit, while also working privately as a life coach, she applies her gift of quiet leadership in everything she does — all of it to serve others, especially women. Michelle is always well prepared, she leads thoughtfully, and she shows respect to all the people she works with, no matter what their position in an organization may be. Michelle has the gift of guiding and empowering people without the need for personal glory and recognition. She reminds me that in order to be a leader, it is not necessary to be the loudest or the pushiest person in the room.

The 50/50 Friendship Flow Challenge Lesson: There is great power in being a quiet leader.

The 50/50 Friendship Flow Challenge to Take Action: Think about what being a quiet leader means to you — both at home and at work. Decide that you'll begin expressing these qualities.

Journal

Today's date is:

I can be effective as a quiet leader — both at home and at work — by leading in the following ways:

A strong leader lets go of ego and allows opportunities to arise for everyone.

Chapter 13

Cultivate a Curious Mind

Date 13 — March 11, 2019, Monday
JOEY Southcenter, Tukwila, Washington
Lunch
Girlfriend: Michelle

Michelle and I met approximately 12 years ago at a mixed martial arts studio in Seattle, Washington. Her youthful appearance belies the fact that she is in her early 50s. While we talked a bit at the school, I think we really became instantly comfortable with each other when we realized that we are both of Korean ancestry. We found our common experience in our cultural identities.

Time flies when I am with Michelle. When we met for our 50/50 Friendship Flow Challenge date, I announced that before we ate, I had to stop my fasting app. Just a few days prior to our date, I had started the 16/8 fasting diet. Michelle responded by sharing that she had recently started fasting as a way of daily living, too. Of course, we laughed at the coincidence. Every time we are together, we naturally start sharing articles that we have read, books that we have found interesting, and any bits of knowledge that we have picked up since the last time we were together.

Our conversation during our lunch naturally flowed into why I had asked Michelle to be one of my 50/50 Friendship Flow Challenge dates. I enjoyed sharing with her what she brings to my life and who she inspires me to be. I describe Michelle as a seeker and a finder. I admire her non-stop yearning for knowledge, and her constant drive to grow and strive to be the best version of herself. When Michelle shares information with me or shares a reference that I should look into, regardless of the topic, I find myself taking out my iPhone to jot down notes. She reminds me to cultivate my curious nature and to appreciate the constant opportunities for growth, learning, and exploration that exist every single day.

The 50/50 Friendship Flow Challenge Lesson: Cultivate a curious mind.

The 50/50 Friendship Flow Challenge to Take Action: Sign up for a class, join a group, grab a book to read, or listen to a podcast on a subject that you are curious about. In this way, you'll continue to grow, learn, and explore.

Journal

Todays date is:

_____

This week, I will pick up a new book, join a class, or listen to a podcast on a new subject. Here's a list of what I have been curious to learn more about lately.

_____

_____

_____

_____

_____

_____

_____

_____

_____

_____

_____

_____

A mind needs constant and consistent exercise for cognitive health and overall wellbeing. Remain curious, and you'll never stop learning and growing.

Chapter 14

Understand Where You
Came From

Date 14 — March 13, 2019, Wednesday
Water's Table, Renton, Washington
Dinner
Girlfriend: Imelda

O ut of all of my 50/50 Friendship Flow Challenge dates, I have known Imelda the longest. She and I grew up just four houses away from one another. As children, we lived in a very culturally diverse neighborhood in South Seattle. We were just two years of age when we met. Her older brother, Artemio, was walking around our neighborhood with her. Artemio may have been five years old at the time, but that is what parents did back in the day. Their preschoolers were free range; parents did not helicopter their kids. Imelda is from an immigrant family — her parents immigrated from the Philippines to the United States with seven kids in tow. She is the only girl in the family, and the youngest. Our birthdays are just three days apart. When we were children — not quite understanding the birds and the bees at that age — I found our close birth dates to be something special, announcing to her that if she had been born three days later or I three days earlier, we would have been twins.

Even though we grew up just four houses away from each other, Imelda and I attended different schools from second grade on. My parents, who were deeply religious, pulled me out of the public school system and placed me in a Christian K–8 school. Imelda would also eventually leave the public school system for a few years, attending a Catholic school. She returned to the public school system in high school where she met the love of her life. She and her husband married shortly after high school and started a family. While she was starting life as a young mother, I went away to college and then to law school. Imelda and I have ebbed and flowed out of each other's lives, but always, whenever we see each other, we pick up right where we left off, as childhood friends do.

It was not until adulthood, after being invited to several parties at her home, that I grasped how close she is to her family and to her Filipino community. As a kid, I knew that she was of Filipino ancestry, and I saw that her home was always filled with aunts, uncles, and cousins — at least that's how she described them. What I did not realize was that throughout her childhood, her parents were creating a strong sense of identity for her by exposing her to her Filipino roots.

During our 50/50 Friendship Flow Challenge date, I explained that I have been impressed by her strong sense of identity — something I did not really gain for myself until well into adulthood. Without hesitation, she agreed that she has always had a strong sense of knowing who she is. She has always known where she came from. Imelda reminds me that it is important not just to know my roots, but also to fully accept and to be wholly conscious of where I came from. In this way, with gratitude, I can totally accept and appreciate who I am today.

The 50/50 Friendship Flow Challenge Lesson: Understanding and accepting where you came from is the first ingredient to being altogether comfortable in your own skin.

The 50/50 Friendship Flow Challenge to Take Action: Take a moment to write down five childhood family memories or daily family rituals that shaped who you are today.

Journal

Today's date is:

_____

I am who I am in part because of my family and cultural history, namely:

_____

_____

_____

_____

_____

_____

_____

_____

_____

_____

_____

_____

_____

_____

Where you are from is a piece of the puzzle to who you are today.

"Your challenges are not a disadvantage. Instead, facing your challenges and overcoming them is actually one of your biggest advantages."

—Shari Leid

Chapter 15

Put a Lil' More Effort into Your Friendships

Date 15 — March 18, 2019, Monday
Beach Café, Kirkland, Washington
Dinner
Girlfriend: Shelley

I met Shelley when she was just 21 years old and I was 37. I was fortunate enough to have made an appointment at a new skincare spa, and as luck would have it, I was placed on Shelley's books. She has been my aesthetician for over 12 years now. Over the past 12 years, I have grown up with her. Because of our age difference, it may be easy to assume that when I say I grew up with her that I mean I have watched her grow. While that is true, it is equally true that *she* has watched *me* grow.

Through her actions, Shelley teaches me how to be a better friend. While making friends and starting new relationships has been something that fortunately I have never struggled with, what I have learned from Shelley is the importance of telling friends — especially long- term friends — how much they mean to me. She models ideal friendship, without competition. She demonstrates by example how to nurture friendships, showing that just a little more effort, to make a friend feel special, goes a long way. She does this with simple acts of kindness, which can come in the form of a handwritten card, special decorations laid out on a restaurant table for a friend's birthday, or even a text sent at the right time.

I told Shelley at our dinner that as a recipient of many of her small acts of kindness over the years, I've recognized that she has given me a life-changing gift. I have followed her lead and paid it forward in my other friendships, which I know has strengthened many of my relationships. In turn, her example has not only brought me more happiness but also spread more happiness to the people around me. And I hope they are paying it forward, too.

The 50/50 Friendship Flow Challenge Lesson: Putting a little more effort into your friendships goes a long way towards strengthening those bonds.

The 50/50 Friendship Flow Challenge to Take Action: Now's the time to commit to the 50/50 Friendship Flow Challenge.

Journal

Todays date is:

_____

Here is the list of the people I am committing to meet with over the next year, as I take on the 50/50 Friendship Flow Challenge.

_____

_____

_____

_____

_____

_____

_____

_____

_____

_____

_____

_____

_____

_____

_____

_____

_____

_____

Nurtured relationships are the key to overall happiness and wellbeing.

Chapter 16

Find the Connection Between Your Heart and Your Mind

Date 16 — March 19, 2019, Tuesday

Momiji, Seattle, Washington

Happy Hour

Girlfriend: Michelle

Michelle has the warmest smile. When she smiles, she smiles with her whole face. Her eyes light up when she laughs, and her laughs are big and genuine. She is an intellect and a poet. She has a gift with words. She studied Human Biology at Stanford before moving on to medical school. In an unfamiliar group, she may initially appear as one of the quieter ones, but if you are fortunate enough to strike up a conversation with her, you will find that you'll want to stay with her the entire night. She is brilliant and witty. She is a leader in her field and a woman whom I deeply admire.

Michelle and I met briefly at a girlfriend's birthday dinner four years ago. We were seated at opposite ends of one of those long rectangular tables, so we did not have a chance to talk to each other during the dinner. However, towards the end of the evening before I left the restaurant, I made my way to the other end of the table to introduce myself to several new faces. Michelle was one of them. Although we did not have a chance to talk for very long that evening, we became Facebook friends later that week. The following year, we happened to attend the same Halloween party and we were able to connect there. It was from that party that our friendship easily fell into place.

During the course of my 50/50 Friendship Flow Challenge journey, I attended a weekend seminar which involved a few exercises that required me to voice what I felt. It was during that weekend that I realized how much I live in my head, and what a difficult time I have accessing what's in my heart. I saw during that weekend seminar that more often than not, I actually use my head to define what I feel, rather than my heart. That weekend experience has prompted me to diligently work on developing a stronger head-and-heart connection. As I work on recognizing and trusting my feelings and intuition, I think about the way Michelle lives, integrating her thoughts and feelings with ease. I see her as my role model.

Michelle is an in-patient pediatric physician at our local children's hospital. But I found out that not only is she a practicing physician, she also holds a number of other leadership positions in the community. You may expect that such a woman would live primarily in her head; on the contrary, she is an exceptional woman with an overflowing heart and soul. Michelle is a poet, a physician, a mother, and an advocate for people and causes close to her heart. She brings her creativity and intelligence together seamlessly. Thus her heart and her mind are connected, which makes her not just an outstanding physician, but also a better wife, mother, and friend to all. We are all meant to be both thinkers and feelers.

The 50/50 Friendship Flow Challenge Lesson: For overall wellbeing and growth, it is necessary to connect the heart and the mind. The two cannot thrive separately.

The 50/50 Friendship Flow Challenge to Take Action: Listen to your heart — your gut, your intuition — not just to your thoughts. Actively cultivate your head-and-heart connection.

Journal

Todays date is:

Magic happens when my heart and my mind are in synchronicity.
For example:

The head and the heart become the strongest force of nature
when they connect to work together as one.

"Do not make it your goal to be something. Make it your goal to be someone."

—Shari Leid

Chapter 17

Be an Influencer

Date 17 — March 20, 2019, Wednesday
Anthony's Home Port, Kirkland, Washington
Dinner
Girlfriend: Miriam

It is easy to mistake Miriam for a magazine cover model. She is one of those women who can wear any hair color from blonde to dark brunette and look absolutely fabulous. She is a chameleon, able to pull off a number of different looks flawlessly. A fitness instructor, she's married to a man everyone instantly loves, and she's mom to a middle-school-aged daughter and a grade-school-aged son. She is in her early 40s, incredibly fit, and loves getting glammed up for fun nights out. I believe that when I first met Miriam at a girlfriend's house, she was a blonde. So, when I met her the second time, I did not recognize her because she had become a brunette. Nonetheless, as I tried to figure out who this woman was who clearly recognized me, I finally put two and two together based on her warm heart, sense of humor, and simple friendliness. While Miriam has fun with her hair color, fashion, and make-up, her heart stays the same. She is consistently friendly and kind to everyone she meets.

I knew that Miriam was wondering what I was going to say to her during our 50/50 Friendship Flow Challenge date. She had watched my previous 16 dates unfold online, as I posted each date on Facebook. One thing that she was not expecting me to tell her is that I view her as an effortless, powerful influencer. People are naturally drawn to her. I started noticing a trend after hosting large parties at my home. Without fail, following the party, I would hear from several people who met Miriam for the first time:

"I really loved your friend, Miriam."

"I'd love to get to know your friend Miriam better."

"It would be fun to get together and invite Miriam."

Because Miriam is not an attention seeker or someone who walks into a place immediately talking to everyone she sees, it is hard to pinpoint exactly which quality attracts people so naturally to her. In fact, when she finds herself in an unfamiliar group of people, she can start out as one of the less talkative of the group.

As I prepared for our 50/50 Friendship Flow Challenge date, I focused on what observing her as a genuine influencer has taught me. As I thought of Miriam's power to affect the world, I began to see how I could cultivate my ability to influence the world the way I hope to do. While I described Miriam's outer beauty, I comprehend that the power she holds comes from who she is inside. By living authentically, her inside beauty radiates. Her sincerity allows her to be an influencer effortlessly — something that we can all be, once we let go of trying to be someone we are not. Once we become comfortable in our own skin, free to play with our outside appearance if it suits us, while remaining consistent with who we are on the inside, we all can be the influencers we want to be. Being a true influencer, like Miriam, comes without effort; it happens when you shine from the inside.

The 50/50 Friendship Flow Challenge Lesson: True influencers are women whose power springs from the fact that they are living their authentic life.

The 50/50 Friendship Flow Challenge to Take Action: Decide today to be your real self; live an authentic life.

Journal

Today's date is:

_____

I am a natural influencer when I live authentically. Here's how I do it.

_____

_____

_____

_____

_____

_____

_____

_____

_____

_____

_____

_____

_____

We all have the power to be an influencer in our community —
by simply being our true self.

"Every small act of kindness
adds beauty to the world."
—Shari Leid

Chapter 18

Proceed with Diplomacy

Date 18 — March 22, 2019, Friday
The Fireside Lounge, Woodinville, Washington
Happy Hour
Girlfriend: Erin

Erin is a tall, blonde, blue-eyed woman in her late 40s. With her husband, she has a blended family of seven children ranging in age from the early 20s to a very active preschooler. Erin is athletic, and able to pick up new sports with ease. She is someone I can text to about anything — whether it be something I see that makes me laugh or something I need to gripe about. I can text her day or night, and I know I will get a response. Erin and I have known each other for over ten years. When I think of the lessons I have learned from my friendship with Erin, her gift for diplomacy stands out to me.

diplomacy: <noun> The art of dealing with people in a sensitive and effective way.

As I mentioned, I am able to reach out to Erin at any given time. She and I can text or talk to one another, be completely at wits' end about someone or some situation, bitch and laugh, and then figure out what roles we played in the situation. Not only that; we further the discussion by texting or talking through ways in which we could do better.

While I myself make the attempt to show diplomacy with others, Erin takes it to a whole new level. She has the gift of being able to effectively process her emotions while in the midst of conflict, to the point where she can recognize her own role in the matter. She then quickly knows just how to proceed with compassion and grace. She reminds me that I bear responsibility, and that I always have choices in every situation. I am never a victim.

While it sounds cliché to say *I love doing life* with Erin, I really do — because it is not just doing, it is growing and learning together, understanding the role we play in every relationship and in every situation, which allows us to proceed through any tough moment with diplomacy.

The 50/50 Friendship Flow Challenge Lesson: Recognizing the role you play in every conflict will allow you to proceed with diplomacy.

The 50/50 Friendship Flow Challenge to Take Action: Analyze your role in a current conflict that you are experiencing. Remember that you control only your own actions, and not the actions of others. Determine how you can resolve each conflict with diplomacy.

Journal

Today's date is:

While I cannot control many situations, I do control my own actions and
reactions. My choice to move forward in a conflict with diplomacy will
transform the circumstances. For instance:

----

*The only thoughts and actions that you can control
are your own.*

"Each time we lift up another woman, we lift up all women."

—Shari Leid

"No one can make you feel
inferior without your consent."
— Eleanor Roosevelt

Chapter 19

Focus on Quality over Quantity

Date 19 — March 25, 2019, Monday
Central Bar + Restaurant, Bellevue, Washington
Lunch
Girlfriend: Kathy

Kathy is a tall, beautiful Black American woman. She has light-colored eyes and shoulder-length hair. She and I were childhood best friends from second grade through eighth grade, only to be separated by attending different high schools. Her parents sent her to a Catholic school and mine sent me to a Christian school, which would turn out to be one of many high schools that I would attend. She has an adult son who graduated not too long ago from college, and she and her husband reside in her childhood home.

The gift of sharing a childhood with someone and having the opportunity to sit down together and reflect on those precious years is priceless. We lost touch for many years following eighth grade, not having the luxury of social media to stay connected. Fortunately, we were able to find each other on Facebook, so now for the last five years, we have a made it a point to get together at least once a year to catch up on life.

It is always fun to reminisce about our experiences as kids. Needless to say, Kathy and I are not the same people we were as children. It is fascinating to witness our growth and our journeys after eighth grade, a time when we were inseparable at school.

What impresses me as I look at Kathy now is how she keeps her friendship circle tight. That is, relationships she commits time to are important to her. It is not necessary for her to have a circle of hundreds of acquaintances; it means much more to her to have a smaller circle of meaningful relationships.

As someone who has a history of casting a wide net and running all over the place getting together with a million people in a day, I appreciate her ability to put her energies towards a smaller group of people — to individuals who really make a difference in her life and who mean something special to her. I am impressed with Kathy's ability to form bonds. Those who find themselves in her circle of friends feel very honored to be her friend.

I am fortunate to have had a childhood best friend in Kathy, who set an example for me early in life of what forming solid bonds with others looks like. Having her as such an important presence in my life, being one half of our duo, certainly gave me a lot of self-confidence and comfort throughout those awkward and challenging grade-school and middle-school years. And now, three and a half decades later, I am thankful to once again be a part of her circle. I am thankful for the reminder: It is not the *quantity* of friendships that matters; it's the *quality* that is important.

The 50/50 Friendship Flow Challenge Lesson: It is better to have five true friendships than ten superficial ones.

The 50/50 Friendship Flow Challenge to Take Action: Work on increasing the quality of your friendships, not the quantity. Set a dinner date with your BFF.

Journal

Today's date is:

_____

I am thankful for my one-of-a-kind ride-or-die girlfriends. Here's a list.
And here's why.

_____

_____

_____

_____

_____

_____

_____

_____

_____

_____

_____

_____

*Quantity without quality means nothing when it
comes to relationships.*

"You are a kind, talented, and unique woman."

—Shari Leid

Chapter 20

Shine from Within

Date 20 — March 27, 2019, Wednesday
Starbucks, Madison Park, Seattle, Washington
Tea
Girlfriend: Suzanne

It is hard to believe that Suzanne and I have been friends for over a decade now. As we sat down for tea during our 50/50 Friendship Flow Challenge date, we shared stories of our kids and caught up on our busy lives. Both of us found that we were each in the midst of college searches with our high-school juniors, which included planned trips to the east coast during Spring Break to tour a number of schools. We contemplated our upcoming travels and the college search process, both looking forward to hearing reports of which schools each of our kids would choose.

I have never before had the occasion to use the term *understated elegance*, but as I thought about Suzanne prior to our 50/50 Friendship Flow Challenge date, that's the phrase that came to mind. While some women work incredibly hard to stand out in a crowd with hair, make-up, and bodycon outfits, Suzanne has a style that is always on point. She presents herself perfectly for the occasion, classically trendy, but never overly done. She is comfortable without make-up and confident in her own skin. As I told her, if anything, she downplays her social status and never boasts of the career that she had prior to choosing to be a stay-at-home mom. She never flaunts where she lives (which happens to be in one of the most highly sought-after secured Seattle communities); she doesn't brag about her many talents and successes.

My 50/50 Friendship Flow Challenge lesson from Suzanne is that when I present myself with an understated elegance, I convey an energy of secure confidence and trustworthiness. I am reminded that rather than trying to get noticed because of my status or physical appearance, focusing on sharing who I am on the inside by radiating an understated elegance will allow my true spirit to shine through.

The 50/50 Friendship Flow Challenge Lesson: True elegance does not take work.

The 50/50 Friendship Flow Challenge to Take Action: Without pretense, simply be yourself. You will shine.

Journal

Today's date is:

_____

I am imperfectly perfect —— I'm just right with all my flaws. Here's how
I will shine from within as my best self, with my own understated elegance:

_____

_____

_____

_____

_____

_____

_____

_____

_____

_____

_____

_____

There is only one you. Celebrate yourself!

Chapter 21

Make the First Move

Date 21 — March 28, 2019, Thursday
Seattle Yacht Club, Seattle, Washington
Dinner
Girlfriend: Tracey

How did Tracey and I meet? She made the first move. Tracey and I kept appearing on each other's Facebook "People You May Know" sidebar. This is the social media sidebar where the same faces and names appear so often, at some point they become so familiar that you start to think that you must know them. Tracey noticed that we share many mutual friends — and not just virtual friends but real flesh-and-blood mutual friends — so she reached out to me. Tracey sent a friend request, and then in true Tracey style, she messaged me to explain that with all our mutual friends, it was surprising that we had not yet met. In fact, looking over our mutual friend list, we were both quite surprised.

While reaching out to introduce herself was incredibly kind, the life lesson I learned from Tracey came later, a little over a year prior to our 50/50 Friendship Flow Challenge date, still a couple of months before we actually met in person. It happened during one of my most vulnerable days.

I do not recall the reason for my appointment at Seattle Cancer Care Alliance, but it was an important one. It was either for an MRI, a results meeting, or something similar, which felt big and scary. I planned on attending the appointment alone because historically when things happen, despite their magnitude, I usually just handle it. However, I woke up the morning of my appointment feeling vulnerable. I realized I did not want to be alone. I wrote a Facebook post saying, "I'm thinking that it wasn't the best plan for me to go to this appointment alone."

Tracey was one of the first persons to respond. This woman whom I'd never met in person tells me that she can drop everything, pick me up (and I live in an entirely different city, probably 45 minutes away from her), take me to my appointment (which would have added another 45-minute drive back to the city), and then drive me back home. While I did not take her up on the offer, this act of kindness has stood out to me on a very high level. I reflect on her actions often.

What I've learned from Tracey:

1. Never think that I shouldn't be the one to volunteer to help because I am not close enough to the person in need;

2. Simple acts of kindness can have a profound impact; and

3. Never be afraid to make the first move to begin a friendship. Life is too short.

The 50/50 Friendship Flow Challenge Life Lesson: Never allow the fear of being rejected stop you from making the first move to begin a new relationship.

The 50/50 Friendship Flow Challenge to Take Action: If there's someone you would like to be friends with, make the first move.

Journal

Today's date is:

_____

I am interested in developing a friendship and I will make the first move with:

_____

_____

_____

_____

_____

_____

_____

_____

_____

_____

_____

_____

_____

We are all members of the human race. Don't be shy. Be kind.
Make the first move, and make a new friend.

"You can't move forward if you
keep looking back."
—Shari Leid

Chapter 22

Focus on the Essence
of a Person

Date 22 — March 30, 2019, Saturday
Revolve Food & Wine, Bothell, Washington
Brunch
Girlfriend: Laverne

L averne and I met over ten years ago through our aesthetician — something that probably happens much more in places like Los Angeles than in Seattle, so I consider us lucky. Laverne has become one of my closest friends.

Over the years, I have noticed that Laverne surrounds herself with people of incredibly good character, which does not occur by accident. Laverne is attracted to the essence of a person. To see someone's essence is to see a person's core nature, or most important quality. There is an anonymous quote that I've always loved: "If only our eyes saw souls instead of bodies, how very different our ideals of beauty would be." While Laverne's friends are all physically beautiful in their own right, the common thread that I have experienced when meeting her friends is that I have an immediate sense that I am meeting a person of depth — someone with an incredibly good heart, and with an authenticity that is welcoming and without judgment.

It is so easy to be seduced by wealth, popularity, and other external factors. But Laverne stays true to her values, forming relationships based on the essence of a person, not on appearances — and this is a quality that I truly admire in her. I constantly try to mirror her example in my life. Because of Laverne, I appreciate that being able to focus on the essence of a person allows me to develop relationships on a deeper level, forming friendships based on an authentic heartfelt connection. Laverne reminds me to see the beauty that resides in each of us.

The 50/50 Friendship Flow Challenge Lesson: Physical beauty, job status, and money all fade, but internal strength stays forever.

The 50/50 Friendship Flow Challenge to Take Action: Look past the outward appearance, and focus instead on the essence of the people around you.

Journal

Today's date is:

I see the inner beauty of the people with whom I surround myself. This is what I notice:

Inner beauty lasts forever.

Chapter 23

Elevate the Room

Date 23 — April 16, 2019, Tuesday
Seattle Tennis Club, Seattle, Washington
Dinner
Girlfriend: Dana

One of the most amazing compliments I have received in recent years is, "I can't believe you have never met Dana, because you remind me of her." My first thought at this comment was *How could I possibly remind you of this beautiful woman who looks like a high-fashion model — pre–Bobby Brown Whitney — a woman who is so incredibly dynamic?* Dana is not simply beautiful, she is smart and witty, with a far-reaching social circle. She is a successful businesswoman dedicated to her family, which includes her adult son who not only has unmistakable natural leadership skills but who also works side by side with her as her trusted business partner. Dana is also mom to a beautiful daughter, who currently attends college in California — a gifted speaker, writer, athlete and caring friend to all.

I finally met Dana about two years ago. It took me a little while to figure out what our mutual friend saw in us that prompted her to tell me that I reminded her of Dana. Then I got to know who Dana allows into her life — and it is everyone. She and I both have a very large, diverse circle of friends, and we both love people from the instant we meet them. We do not discriminate based on race, income, or social status. This quality is what our mutual friend saw in us.

Dana, though, takes it to the next level. At our 50/50 Friendship Flow Challenge date, I told her that she is "the garnish." What I mean by that is, she elevates a room simply by being present. When people find out that Dana is attending a meeting or an event, the gathering is elevated to something special. Guests know that whatever they are attending will be remarkable, in part because Dana will be there. Her energy, her smile, and her effortless communication style all put the whole room at ease.

She shared with me that when she wakes up in the morning, she sets intentions. She realizes her blessings. She also remembers the hardships of the people around her. And, she shows up equally for everyone. She shows up for the one-percenters and she shows up for the 99-percenters in the same way. There is a social media post that people often like to share on Facebook, which says something to the effect of the importance of treating the janitor and the CEO the same. I have not seen Dana share this quote, but I have certainly seen her live it.

The lesson I've learned from Dana is to show up completely with everyone who crosses my path each day. By being fully present at any gathering I attend, I can also be "the garnish" — I can be that person who elevates the room.

The 50/50 Friendship Flow Challenge Lesson: Treat everyone the same. Be welcoming to all.

The 50/50 Friendship Flow Challenge to Take Action: Find someone outside of your social circle, and take time to talk to that person; you're guaranteed to learn something fascinating.

Journal

Today's date is:

_____

I intend to be "the garnish" — living with the intention to elevate others wherever I go. Here's how I'll do it:

_____

_____

_____

_____

_____

_____

_____

_____

_____

_____

_____

_____

We are all souls having a human experience. Each of us just wants to be recognized.

"It is never too late to start a new relationship, a new career, a new outlook."

—Shari Leid

Chapter 24

Believe You Can

Date 24 — April 17, 2019, Wednesday
The Matador, Tacoma, Washington
Happy Hour
Girlfriend: Celia

Celia is the daughter of a Mexican-American mother and a European-American father. She has thick, dark curly hair that falls below her shoulders, and she is fair in complexion with light hazel eyes and dimples to die for. Celia identifies as a Latina woman, as she was raised in a Mexican-American community of friends in an area of California which she calls "Calexico." She is a successful business owner, attorney, and community leader. She is also a gifted communicator. Hands down, Celia is a self-made woman, and mother to an adult son whom she adores. I am blown away by her success, her work ethic, her drive, and her incredible intelligence.

Celia and I met several years ago when I was practicing law and she was a law student. As a law student she joined the Pierce County Minority Bar Association in Tacoma, Washington, an association of which I was an active member. Since there were just a handful of racial minority attorneys and law students in the Tacoma area at the time, it was easy to get to know every person in our tiny bar. After I moved up to Seattle to practice, we lost touch for a bit, but thanks to Facebook, we reconnected and have been able to see each other at least twice a year for the past few years. By the time we reconnected, Celia had gone from law student to an extremely well-respected attorney.

Her story is inspiring. When Celia began law school, she was a single mother with a young child. Not only did she manage to work part-time through most of law school, raising a child on her own (including finding a daycare close to the school since she lived in another city), she was also active in school organizations and professional organizations while a law student. Upon graduation she opened a personal injury litigation practice, and she now has two busy offices. She employs an associate attorney, contract attorneys, and staff. Celia has continued to be an active leader in professional organizations, and does more *pro bono* work than your average attorney. Personal Injury Litigation is an area that is still dominated by men, with an even lower representation of attorneys of color. Therefore, for Celia to be so successful as a Latina woman in this field is truly phenomenal.

I met with her for our 50/50 Friendship Flow Challenge date to find out what the driving force is that has not only led her to survive but also to thrive. I asked her what impels her to succeed. How did she raise a young child as a single mom, attend law school, and work, and become active in her community? Her initial response was that there was no choice. It is who she is. Simple enough. But she did have a choice. She could have looked at the road in front of her and decided that it was too difficult. She could have decided that law school was not an option for a single mom who did not have financial means. She could have decided that opening up her own law practice was too risky. She could have decided that *pro bono* work should be left to other attorneys. But she did not.

Celia was driven to succeed because she decided that for her, there was no other choice. Celia demonstrates the way I wish to live, and the way I hope my kids will live. The old adage, "If there is a will, there is a way" is not just empty words. If you ever think that something appears impossible for you, think of Celia and be inspired. She is brilliant, driven, and compassionate — an absolutely beautiful human being.

The 50/50 Friendship Flow Challenge Lesson: You can do anything you set your mind to. If there's a will, there's a way.

The 50/50 Friendship Flow Challenge to Take Action: What have you been avoiding doing because you thought you couldn't really do it? You *can* do it. Take a step towards doing it today.

Journal

Today's date is:

_____

Here's what I've been putting off, but now I know I can do it. Here are the steps I'll take:

_____

_____

_____

_____

_____

_____

_____

_____

_____

_____

_____

_____

_____

Removing limiting thoughts allows a sea of opportunity
to flow your way. Believe you can, and you will.

Chapter 25

Embrace Life's Constant Flow of Change

Date 25 — April 22, 2019, Monday

Central Bar + Restaurant, Bellevue, Washington

Dinner

Girlfriend: Natalie

Natalie is a photographer, a wife, and a mother to three sons — an adult son, a college-aged son, and a high-school-aged son. She is a talented photographer, gifted in shooting everyday women to bring out their strength and beauty through her lens. Natalie is also incredibly talented in capturing amazing commercial shots for her business and media clients. She has not only an artistic eye but also a keen business sense.

Because her life is in continuous flux, Natalie reminds me that really, the only constant in life is change. No matter what she commits herself to, she masters it. She is never stagnant. She treats life as the adventure it is meant to be. She is not afraid to stop and change direction. She has developed the knack to swerve in another direction when a change calls for it. She is not afraid to experiment, challenge herself, and to learn from experience.

Natalie reminds me that changes mean opportunities for growth. She shows me that I am not the only one who is changing and growing — everyone around me is doing the same. Being aware that everyone around me is also in constant change and growth allows me to resolve conflicts. While I am not the same person I was a year ago, a month ago, or even a week ago, it is good to remember that any person whom I have had a conflict with in the past is not the same person today, either. I can see clearly that it is important for me to acknowledge and allow change and growth in others. I am so fortunate to be in this flow of life with Natalie. I cannot wait to see where our roads and detours take us.

The 50/50 Friendship Flow Challenge Lesson: Life is in a constant flow of change.

The 50/50 Friendship Flow Challenge to Take Action: Give yourself permission to swerve in another direction when necessary. Every change is an opportunity for learning and growth.

Journal

Today's date is:

_____

Here's an area where I know I need to swerve in another direction because
of a change. I will do so now, giving myself permission to learn and grow.

_____

_____

_____

_____

_____

_____

_____

_____

_____

_____

_____

_____

_____

*Life's path is not a straight and narrow line; it is an exciting
road with many twists and turns.*

Chapter 26

Share Small Acts of Kindness

Date 26 — April 23, 2019, Tuesday
JOEY Bellevue, Bellevue, Washington
Happy Hour
Girlfriend: Cindy

It is the little things that build trust and longevity in a relationship. It does not matter what type of relationship it is — a friendship, a marriage, or a professional relationship. It is the little things that add up.

Shortly after I met Cindy, we found ourselves at a small gathering at a friend's home, and it happened to be the day after I had experienced a very difficult encounter. Cindy heard my story and the discussion that followed among our mutual friends. To my surprise, the next day I received an email from Cindy. It began with, "While we barely know each other..." and ended with, "If you ever need someone to talk to...."

I told Cindy that I have never forgotten that simple act of kindness. Over the years, she has been that friend I can count on. She is the friend who texts to check in on me and to follow up when she knows that I may be dealing with a challenge, which in most recent years was my battle with breast cancer. She shows her constant support by simply being present. It is her small, consistent acts of kindness that remind me that she is always there for me. She shows me that strong relationships are based on trust, and trust is built by making sure that the other person knows you are there on a dependable basis. It is not a grand, one-time showing up; it is dependable support. It does not take money or extravagant gifts to build the foundation of a strong relationship; it takes the giving of your time. Simply taking the time to send a quick text is often enough to remind people that you are there for them.

Following Cindy's lead, I plan to consciously build and strengthen my friendships, with small, reliable acts of support and kindness, knowing that these acts will add up to large returns in the quality of all of my relationships.

The 50/50 Friendship Flow Challenge Lesson: It is the little things that count.

The 50/50 Friendship Challenge to Take Action: Text or call someone today, simply to let that person know you are thinking about them.

Journal

Todays date is:

- -

Small acts of kindness do not cost a thing. This week, I will reach out to the
following friends, just to check in to let them know Im thinking about them.

- -

- -

- -

- -

- -

- -

- -

- -

- -

- -

- -

- -

Its the little things you do that make a big difference.

Chapter 27

Live Independently in the Now

Date 27 — April 29, 2019, Monday
McMenamins Elks Temple, Tacoma, Washington
Happy Hour
Girlfriend: Tanya

Tanya and I met when we were 24 years old, which means that we have known each other for more than half of our lives. While we worked together and we were really close friends in our mid-20s, life happened, so we found ourselves going through much of our late 20s, 30s, and early 40s with little contact. The scant contact was not due to any fallout, but just because we lived in two different cities, over an hour away from each other. Fortunately for both of us, during the years that we were apart, we were not stagnant. Both of us came out of all the craziness that the 20s bring, unscathed. We grew up. We became adults. We became wives and mothers.

As I look back to who we were in our 20s as opposed to who we are now, a lot has changed; but one thing that has not changed is Tanya's fierce independence. Tanya's mom died when she was only 21 years old, at a time when she was working to pay for tuition and living expenses while attending college as a full-time student. As life's timing often does, her mom's death also coincided with the end of a serious romantic relationship. During that difficult time, Tanya made a conscious choice, recognizing that she could choose the easy path and become self-destructive or she could choose the more difficult path of moving forward. She told me that she remembers the night when she was alone in her college living quarters, and she chose the more difficult path. At that young age, she decided that her past would not hold her back, nor would any fears of the future. Tanya chose to live in the now.

Shortly after college, still in her 20s, Tanya moved to Washington State after a lifetime of living in Michigan. Living alone several states from home, at age 24 she became a Supervisor in the Victims Advocate Unit of the Pierce County Prosecutor's Office, not afraid to stand up to much older — mostly male — attorneys to voice the rights of the victims for whom she was responsible. Most recently, Tanya again showed her independence by going back to school in her 40s and becoming a licensed therapist in Pierce

County, Washington. Now with her own practice, she continues to inspire others to be the best they can be.

During our 50/50 Friendship Flow Challenge date, I shared with Tanya that one of my wishes for my kids is that they will have the self-awareness to let go of messages from the past that do not serve them, that they will have the courage not to fear the future, and that they will possess the independence to live in the now — as I saw her do from the tender age of 21.

The 50/50 Friendship Flow Challenge Lesson: It does no one any good to fear the future; live independently in the now.

The 50/50 Friendship Flow Challenge to Take Action: Let go of any past messages that don't serve you anymore; it's time to write new messages for yourself.

Journal

Todays date is:

_____

I choose to live only with these positive messages, which serve me now:

_____

_____

_____

_____

_____

_____

_____

_____

_____

_____

_____

_____

_____

_____

Independence and freedom are my birthrights.

"Feel the uniqueness of every single day."
—Shari Leid

"With the new day come new strengths and new thoughts."
— Eleanor Roosevelt

Chapter 28

Live Consciously

Date 28 — May 5, 2019, Sunday
Little Water Cantina, Seattle, Washington
Dinner
Girlfriend: Tee-Ta

Tee-Ta is in her late 40s, a Black woman, and relatively tall. She walks into a room with an aura of confidence and beauty. She built and developed her own branding firm from the ground up. Because she lives her life mindfully and intentionally, she is able to help her clients become fully aware of their own identity, to identify exactly who their customers are, and to successfully communicate their business message in the most effective way.

Tee-Ta has an energy about her that screams *fun*. It is not surprising that when Tee-Ta ventured to the ladies' room during our 50/50 Friendship Flow Challenge date, she was met by a group of women who had been seated a few tables away from us. These women actually gushed to her that they noticed her beauty — her unstoppable presence — throughout the whole restaurant. It's not uncommon for Tee-Ta to receive random texts, messages, and social media tags — from people who know her and from some who do not — communications which often share with her their gratitude for inspiring them. I believe the reason for this directness is that Tee-Ta is always transparent and open in the way she shares her personal life journey. She receives expressions of gratitude so often because anyone who observes the way she lives can see that she lives consciously. She has taken control of her life, making decisions that create the life she wants to live rather than simply settling for the life that befalls her. She is fully aware of who she is, and she is totally comfortable in her own skin. She lets go of ego, which allows her to see the world as a place filled with opportunities.

Like everyone who comes in contact with Tee-Ta, I am inspired. I absolutely appreciate being able to walk side by side with a woman who lives consciously, a woman who recognizes not only her own purpose, but the fact that every single person has a unique life purpose. Watching Tee-Ta live her life so deliberately, I am reminded that I, too, have the choice to create the life I want — by living with purpose each moment of any given day.

The 50/50 Friendship Flow Challenge Lesson: When we let go of ego and live life with purpose, any moment can be an opportunity to experience joy.

The 50/50 Friendship Flow Challenge to Take Action: Choose to be mindful, living consciously each and every moment of your life.

Journal

Today's date is:

I choose to live consciously throughout the day today, noticing here my
moments of joy:

----

*Choosing to live authentically is not a one-time decision;
it is an ongoing conscious choice.*

"Do what you've always
wanted to do."
—Shari Leid

50/50 FRIENDSHIP FLOW CHALLENGE

TESTIMONIAL

Miriam Cicero, Fitness Instructor, Kirkland, Washington
(Shari's Date 17)

As I strutted down the sidewalk in my stilettos, I felt oddly nervous, like *first-date nervous*. What was Shari going to say to me? What had she seen in me? Would I like what she had to say? My thoughts and heart racing, I made my way to our table on the patio overlooking Lake Washington. We hugged, we laughed, we chatted, we took windblown selfies, and laughed some more while we waited for our drinks.

Somewhere in that happy-hour whirlwind the conversation got a little more serious, and she asked me why I thought she'd picked me for her 50/50 Friendship Flow Challenge date. I don't remember my response. But I do remember what she said to me because it had a monumental impact (so much so, I still think about it a year later on a daily basis). She said I was the "most influential." *What*?! I felt like I'd just been nominated for class valedictorian! I didn't really believe her, and right off the bat I could think of a handful of friends who fit the title better than me. But I was — then and now — honored and completely humbled by this experience.

I now believe even more than I ever did that people come into our lives for a reason. And it is up to us to cultivate the friendships that inspire and uplift us, and to learn to let go of the ones that don't. What I love about the 50/50 Friendship Flow Challenge is the power it gives you to make a positive impact on the recipients' day, month, or year — or hell, you might even change their whole life!

Chapter 29

Move Forward

Date 29 — May 7, 2019, Monday
Kirkland Waterfront, Kirkland, Washington
Dinner
Girlfriend: Alanda

Alanda exudes style. Her personal Instagram page has organically transformed into a style-influencer page. She is in her early 30s, with pretty brown hair including perfectly placed blonde highlights. She is always seen donning the latest fashion trends which she is able to put together seamlessly. It is not surprising that she radiates style given that she is a highly sought-after hair stylist, make-up artist, and fashion stylist. She is always surrounded by friends and clients who adore her.

I have known Alanda for over a decade. I met her when I was a client at a Seattle-area blow-out bar for hair. At 17 years my junior, she began as my stylist, and in no time she was managing the salon. Like most people who meet Alanda, I instantly loved her from the first time we met. I saw her remarkable drive, and a light that shone from within her that was way beyond her years.

Over the course of our friendship, I have observed that Alanda always moves forward. She moves ahead in everything — whether in her career or her relationships — she simply and elegantly moves forward without dragging the past along with her. In every friendship, relationship, and work–life situation, she gives 100 percent; but when it is done, when it has run its course, she has the ability to move on without carrying any baggage, and she does so without bitterness.

On our 50/50 Friendship Flow Challenge date, I asked Alanda where her ability to consistently move forward no matter what life throws at her originated. Without hesitation, she shared that her dad dying when she was only in high school, and an extremely close friend dying a few years ago — both in tragic accidents — made her appreciate every moment of life. At a young age, she chose to appreciate every experience. Rather than live in victimhood when her father died, she chose to live life to the fullest, realizing that life is a gift to be experienced. She reminds me not only to keep moving forward, but to do so without dragging my past along with me.

The 50/50 Friendship Flow Challenge Lesson: When life gives you obstacles, you have two choices: either to be stopped by the difficulties, or to move through them and beyond.

The 50/50 Friendship Flow Challenge to Take Action: Choose to move forward, without bringing anger or resentment along with you.

Journal

Today's date is:

_____

I choose to let go of the past and move forward with:

_____

_____

_____

_____

_____

_____

_____

_____

_____

_____

_____

_____

_____

_____

_____

_____

It is impossible to move forward if bitterness and resentment are your companions.

"Make time for yourself, daily."

—Shari Leid

Chapter 30

Support Your Friends through Thick and Thin

Date 30 — May 11, 2019, Saturday
Bumpy's, Puyallup, Washington
Brunch
Girlfriend: Carey

Carey and I chose to meet for our 50/50 Friendship Flow Challenge date at a dive bar about 40 minutes south of Seattle. Where else would you get together with a woman you first met in bartending school? Several years ago, Carey and I both signed up for a bartending course as a fun way to learn to mix drinks for our own parties. The biggest takeaway we got from the course was the friendship we developed. Since then, we've made it a point to meet up at least once a year at a dive bar. It's our thing.

Carey is about my size — neither of us is intimidating in stature. She has a youthful appearance, looking much younger than her 50 years of age. While some of the dive bars we have visited may not appear to be the safest spots for two women to enter into alone, I would go to just about any place with Carey, because I know she has my back.

That is Carey. She is fiercely loyal. She values integrity, reliability, and fairness. She gives the people in her life 100 percent. She accepts her friends despite their imperfections. It takes a lot for Carey to step back and let go of a friendship. Something very destructive would have to occur for her to step away; however, even then, because you had been in her life at one time, if she happened to see you being treated unfairly, she would fight for you.

One of my wishes for my kids is that they find their Carey. I hope they find that one person who, no matter what happens, will never allow them to be treated unfairly. I hope they find that faithful person who sticks up for them when needed, even when and if at a particular moment they are not at their most lovable.

Because of Carey, I know what it feels like to have a friend whom I know will support me through thick and thin. I am able to take my experience with Carey and actively seek to mirror her fierce loyalty in my own relationships with friends.

The 50/50 Friendship Flow Challenge Lesson: It's important to stick up for the people you care about. Everyone needs at least one loyal friend.

The 50/50 Friendship Flow Challenge to Take Action: When it comes to your friends, stand up for what is right — not just when it's easy, but in all circumstances.

Journal

Todays date is:

_____

To support my friends through thick and thin, I will:

_____

_____

_____

_____

_____

_____

_____

_____

_____

_____

_____

_____

_____

_____

Healthy friendships are relationships you can count on no matter what.

"You can accomplish anything that you set your mind to."

—Shari Leid

Chapter 31

Align Your Virtual Life with Your Real Life

Date 31 — May 20, 2019, Monday
Citizen Six, Seattle, Washington
Lunch
Girlfriend: Mary

Mary and I attended the same high school together. Although we were in different grades, and we ran in different social circles, we certainly knew each other because it was a small high school. During recent years, many of us from that school have become social media friends. It is through this medium that I got to know who Mary is. Her social media posts stood out to me.

I have appreciated the honesty that Mary brings to her own self-reflection. She shares her observations of herself with such refreshing candor. She gets frustrated with herself, she laughs at herself, and she celebrates herself. She does not pretend to be someone she is not. Her social media life aligns with her real life. There is no grandstanding. Often her posts are about regular day-to-day situations that come up for all of us, which she shares in a way that makes me pause and smile.

Whenever I consider Mary's social media posts and then see her in person, I am clearly reminded of the attractiveness of being authentic. The fact that she aligns her virtual life with her real life is so important, given the huge role social media plays in our daily lives. Mary reminds me that if I truly wish to live an authentic life, my social media life ought to reflect my real life.

The 50/50 Friendship Flow Challenge Lesson: Authenticity means being your most beautiful self. Your authentic self is your only self.

The 50/50 Friendship Flow Challenge to Take Action: Live authentically: Align your virtual life to your real life.

Journal

Today's date is:

_____

I will make sure my virtual life always aligns with my real life by posting
from the heart, not from ego. For instance:

_____

_____

_____

_____

_____

_____

_____

_____

_____

_____

_____

_____

My real self is my best self. When I express authenticity,
I am my one and only true self.

Chapter 32

Live Passionately

Date 32 — May 22, 2019, Wednesday
Six Seven Restaurant, Edgewater Hotel, Seattle Waterfront
Happy Hour
Girlfriend: Lisa Marie

Lisa Marie is a striking beauty in her early 30s, a fashion designer, and a newlywed. Often seen wearing her own couture creations, her make-up is always perfectly applied. She's not one to shy away from red lips. Lisa Marie definitely makes a statement when she enters a room.

> " Your honeymoon-night lingerie should be your every-night lingerie." — Lisa Marie

Did I get your attention? I hope so, because Lisa Marie got mine. She reminds me to live a passionate life.

I met Lisa Marie approximately 15 years ago. She was my stylist, my visionary, at a Seattle-based boutique designer-couture gown shop. I recognized early on that when I was at the boutique as a client, she paid attention. She saw the real me.

As children, we choose activities that bring us joy. We act on instinct — we live passionately. Unfortunately, early on in our lives, we get the message that living passionately is reckless. We soon feel that to survive, we need to conform. We spend most of our young lives figuring out how to become what society deems as successful. We lose our passion. Then comes adulthood — and most of us by this time have lost our ability to connect with our passion. We often do not even know how to discover what our passion is. But not so for Lisa Marie.

Early on in her career, when Lisa Marie worked at the designer boutique where we met, she spent her days observing brides. She watched them transform as soon as they put on a gown that made them feel beautiful. She saw the way brides picked out their lingerie for their wedding night, something that made them feel sexy. So while still in her 20s, she decided that life should always be lived as a bride. Every day should be a special occasion, and every night should be an opportunity to feel your most sexually attractive, confident self — whether that be in flannels, tank tops, or lacy lingerie. Feeling that you are your most gorgeous self should not be reserved for only one day and evening in time.

Our 50/50 Friendship Flow Challenge date was the first time I'd ever met one on one with Lisa Marie outside of the showroom floor. I was excited to share with her that what she brings to my life is the reminder to live passionately. It feels fabulous to wake up every day and know that today is a day to live with passion.

The 50/50 Friendship Flow Challenge Lesson: Live like a blushing bride every day. Every night, live like it is your honeymoon night.

The 50/50 Friendship Flow Challenge to Take Action: Every day there is something to celebrate. Live each day with passion.

Journal

Today's date is:

_____

I will live each day with passion. Today, I celebrate:

_____

_____

_____

_____

_____

_____

_____

_____

_____

_____

_____

_____

_____

Passion fuels my soul daily.

"Don't underestimate the power of journaling."

—Shari Leid

Chapter 33

Always Assume the Best

Date 33 — June 8, 2019, Saturday
Salt and Iron, Edmonds, Washington
Dinner
Girlfriend: Tammy

I met Tammy over ten years ago. At the time, she was a lead instructor at a Seattle-area martial arts gym where I was a student. In addition to being absolutely beautiful, she is also fierce. At the gym, Tammy's classes were known to be some of the hardest you could take. I was intimidated by everything about her; I made assumptions. I did not put much effort into getting to know Tammy because I had placed her in a category separate from me. I am not sure what the category labels would be, but I just know that in my mind it felt as if we were far apart — in separate categories that did not blend.

Fortunately, however, a few years later I invited Tammy to a party at my home. To my surprise, she came. I remember feeling excited when I learned that she was planning on attending, and surprised that she would venture to the party on her own, taking a chance on meeting new people. It was that night that I recognized what an amazing soul Tammy is. She has one of the biggest hearts for the people in her life. I just love laughing with her. She has become part of our group of five Korean women (all of us, except me, grew up with Korean moms). We all get together at least annually. These are the women who have given me such precious insight into what it may have been like had I not been adopted and instead had grown up with my birth mom.

Without knowing it, Tammy taught me the importance of letting go of assumptions. I have gained a lot from my friendship with Tammy. I am incredibly grateful that I did not allow my misguided assumptions to prevent me from developing our friendship. Now, because of this lesson from Tammy, with every person I meet now, I make a new assumption: I simply assume that we can be the best of friends.

The 50/50 Friendship Flow Challenge Lesson: While you have only one chance to make a first impression, you have many opportunities to dive deeper than that initial perception, if you simply open your heart.

The 50/50 Friendship Flow Challenge to Take Action: Instead of assuming you have nothing in common with someone, assume everyone has the potential to be your friend.

Journal

Todays date is:

_____

I wont allow my initial assumptions to prevent what could be the start of
a beautiful friendship. I recognize the goodness that lives inside all of us.
For example:

_____

_____

_____

_____

_____

_____

_____

_____

_____

_____

_____

Every person I meet has the potential to be my
next very best friend.

"Follow your own path."

—Shari Leid

Chapter 34

Prioritize Self-Care

Date 34 — June 10, 2019, Monday
Cactus, Kirkland, Washington
Lunch
Girlfriend: Rachel

The weather was so lovely on the day I met with Rachel for our 50/50 Friendship Flow Challenge date, that we actually had a chance to sit outside for lunch — something that is rare when you live in the rainy Seattle area. On this beautiful sunny day, Rachel walked up wearing a fabulous pair of aviator sunglasses.

Before I dove into why I wanted to meet up with her, I first asked Rachel for permission to talk to her about a very personal topic. She did not hesitate to allow me to continue. I then proceeded to ask questions about her mom, and she graciously allowed me to explore with her how she managed to move from the devastation of losing her mom just a few years ago to gaining so much strength, positivity, perspective, and awareness from her traumatic loss. Rachel and I both lost a parent when we were in our early 30s — younger than most of our peers.

I never had the privilege of meeting Rachel's mom. Until our 50/50 Friendship Flow Challenge lunch, I knew very little about her. The only thing I did know is that when her mother died, Rachel must have taken on her mom's heart. What I mean by that is that I can feel the love and compassion that Rachel has when she offers help to someone. After Rachel's mom's passing, Rachel started a Facebook group to provide support for people and their families who are diagnosed with triple-negative breast cancer. Due to her own experience, she recognized that a need existed for an online forum where patients and families could gain easy access to information and find support. Triple-negative breast cancer is a devastating diagnosis. Rachel's mom went from a Stage 2 diagnosis to a Stage 4 in just a couple of months, surviving for only 15 months after the initial diagnosis. Unfortunately, her short survival rate is not uncommon for such patients. At the time of our 50/50 Friendship Flow Challenge date neither Rachel nor I was aware of any drugs available to effectively fight this diagnosis. It often strikes at a young age, and it is very aggressive.

I can only imagine the immense comfort and support that have resulted from Rachel's creation of this online space. She inherited an open, loving heart from her mom — an exceptional caring spirit for others. It is a special daughter who takes the loss of her mother, and turns that devastating experience into a way to lessen the suffering of others who are going through the same thing, so they won't have to do it alone.

I asked Rachel what advice she would give to our friends who will inevitably go through losing a parent in the coming years. She simply and quickly responded, "Time." Take the time off of work. Step away from extra commitments. Allow yourself the time you need to spend with your mom or dad. Allow yourself to be okay with stopping your usual activities. During the time of her mom's illness, Rachel was fortunate enough to have taken a lunch meeting with a surgeon, who was not one of her mother's treating physicians but who knew of her mom's diagnosis. He candidly told her that her mom was not going to live beyond three months, and advised that she needed to take the time to be with her. Rachel listened to him, took the time off, and cared for her mom — and he was right. Her mom passed away, almost to the day, three months later. Rachel is so thankful that she was encouraged to take that time.

Listening to Rachel, I understood how true her words are. Even though my dad passed away due to immediate heart failure, and therefore I did not have the luxury of planning for extra time with him prior to his death, I see that I should have taken time after his death. I should have allowed myself the time necessary to grieve, to do all that needs to be done when someone dies, without juggling work or extra commitments that really could have waited or which someone else could have handled.

While taking time off work is a luxury that often cannot be afforded, there are other things that we can let go of. The message today is to give yourself the gift of time when you lose a parent. Give yourself time to enjoy being with your parents before they get sick; then take time to be with them if and when they become sick; finally, allow yourself time to grieve and heal when they are gone. It is no sign of weakness to recognize when you need to change direction and take all the time you need. Being able to recognize what your heart, soul, and mind need is a strength.

The 50/50 Friendship Flow Challenge Lesson: It's vital to prioritize self-care. Take time for yourself.

The 50/50 Friendship Flow Challenge to Take Action: Let go of commitments that do not currently serve your needs.

Journal

Today's date is:

These are some of the ways that I will practice self-care today, and from now on:

Self-care is needed before you can properly care for those you love.

Chapter 35

Support Friends Right Where They Are

Date 35 — June 11, 2019, Tuesday

Central Bar + Restaurant, Bellevue, Washington

Dinner

Girlfriend: Meredith

From the first time I met Meredith, I felt that she was someone I could trust. Meredith walks into a room with so much energy and love that she is instantly memorable. She is a person that even strangers gravitate towards. Meredith is a motivational life coach, a medium, an intuitive, and a professional astrologer. She plainly enjoys helping her clients find their path. Meredith honors the individual journey of each of her clients; she does not tie their journey to her own. She meets all people right where they are.

During our 50/50 Friendship Flow Challenge date, I began sharing information about some of the projects I am involved in. Meredith listened intently and immediately asked, "How can I best support you?" She then proceeded to offer a lot of wisdom — checking in with me as we went along to make sure that her ideas met my needs. She met me right where I was, encouraging me in my personal journey. She reminds me of the importance of supporting my friends right where they are, not where I may want them to be.

The 50/50 Friendship Challenge Lesson: Everyone's journey is personal and unique.

The 50/50 Friendship Flow Challenge to Take Action: Let go of the need to control the people around you. Cheer them on, wherever they are.

Journal

Today's date is:

_____

Today I will let go of my need to control others. By doing so, I will support

my friends right where they are:

_____

_____

_____

_____

_____

_____

_____

_____

_____

_____

_____

_____

My journey is uniquely mine, and your journey is uniquely yours.

Chapter 36

Follow Your Dreams

Date 36 — June 30, 2019, Sunday
Momiji, Seattle, Washington
Dinner
Girlfriend: Chanel

Chanel and I are the same age. She has a raw, edgy look to her. A look that is librarian, rocker, tomboy, and sex kitten all wrapped into one woman. She is a dynamic speaker, a writer, a widow, and a mom to a fabulous high-school-aged son.

When I think of Chanel, I think about moments frozen in time. There are just a few people who come into our lives where we experience particular memories that feel like slow-motion movies, and Chanel is one of those friends for me.

Going back about a decade ago, I ran a small personal training studio, which was set up on the basement floor of my home. Chanel was one of my clients. I had donated a personal training package for an auction fundraiser at a local preschool where my kids had attended a few years earlier. I recall my girlfriend with whom I'd attended the auction telling me a few days later, "You'll love the woman who purchased your training sessions. She is a badass. She saw you at the auction and said, 'If that's the ass I get, I'm buying her training sessions.'" I immediately loved this unknown woman named Chanel.

When I had the opportunity to get to know Chanel, I got to enjoy her humor, and admired her capacity to include words like *f#ck* and *sh*t* without any effort. It made me realize that I was sorely lacking in my ability to properly and effectively drop the *f*-bomb. Things were light. Things were easy.

Then one day, life changed. The weather in Seattle was absolutely gorgeous that afternoon, so I went out for a walk around Seward Park, a large city park. As I walked back towards my home, I saw police activity on the street close to the park, where caution tape had been placed. I arrived back home, turned on my computer, and immediately saw Facebook posts of people trying to get a hold of the wife of a bicyclist who was hit and taken to Harborview Hospital — which is Seattle's Level-I Trauma Center. I soon found out that the woman they were looking for was Chanel.

Chanel's husband was taken off of life support not long after. Chanel was suddenly a single mom of a young child who was just starting kindergarten. As her friend, but not a part of her inner circle, I did not know what to do. Some people seem to be natural comforters, knowing the right words to say and the right things to do, but I have never been one of those people.

Chanel came back into the studio a few days later. Instead of attending the group class that she was in, we set aside time to work out without anyone else in the studio. I held up the martial arts pads for her, and she hit and kicked. She worked out so hard that on one of those days she made herself physically ill. She was getting out the anger, frustration, and pain. It was her time. It was her physical release.

During that time, just after her husband's death, I remember her talking about all of the legal documents, all of the paperwork, all sorts of things, including computer passwords, that she was having to deal with. She said to me in great frustration, "You're a lawyer — why isn't all of this stuff known to people? Why isn't this information out there on a website for people to know that they need to get their *sh*t* together before someone dies?" At the time, I recall feeling uncomfortable and responding with agreement and sympathy, but without any commitment to her idea.

In true Chanel form, she did not let it go. A few weeks later, while working on a standing martial arts bag, she asked, "Well, will I get in trouble if I create a site that has all these forms...like wills...for people? If I create a site that has a checklist of things people need to do to get their *sh*t* together, would I get in trouble because I'm not a lawyer?" Again, I responded with a less than enthusiastic response. But I could see that this was an idea she clearly wasn't going to let go of.

Flash forward a few years: I learned that Chanel had created the website that she had described to me while working out in my studio. The *New York Times* had even published an article about her. Then, flash forward ten years later to 2019, and you'll find that Chanel is everywhere with her book, *What Matters Most: The Get-Your-Sh*t-Together Guide to Wills, Money, Insurance, and Life's "What-Ifs."*

Chanel is one of my 50 dates because of what I've learned from her:

1. When you have an idea and you feel it in your heart, don't let the fact that it is out of your realm of experience or expertise stop you from pursuing your idea to make it a reality. Chanel had never hosted a self-help website, nor was she a public speaker, an expert in life's-end matters, a CPA, a lawyer, or an author. But she let none of these facts stop her. She did not let the messages of self-doubt keep her from bringing her idea to fruition. She has taught me to believe in my ideas, to have faith in their validity, and to proceed with conviction.

2. I had always felt guilty that I did not do enough for her when she was going through the sudden loss of her husband. To my shock, when I told her I was going to attend her book launch, she shared with me that I was mentioned in her book. I had no idea what she could have written, and quite frankly I was nervous that the truth of me not being there enough

would be revealed. The absolute opposite was written. Chanel shared that the time I gave her to work out alone in the studio with just me was important and meaningful to her. This recognition has taught me that we do not necessarily have to make a grand gesture; sometimes just being present and giving someone space is enough. The value of giving someone time and space is priceless.

The 50/50 Friendship Flow Challenge Lesson: Just because you have never done it before does not mean you can't do it now.

The 50/50 Friendship Flow Challenge to Take Action: Start something new — something you have always wanted to do.

Journal

Today's date is:

_____

Each day, I am moving forward on my dream to:

_____

_____

_____

_____

_____

_____

_____

_____

_____

_____

_____

_____

_____

_____

_____

You've got this.

"Be your own muse."

—Shari Leid

Chapter 37

Be Mindful

Date 37 — July 17, 2019, Wednesday

Betty Restaurant & Bar, Seattle, Washington

Dinner

Girlfriend: Sonya

I met Sonya this past year at a birthday celebration happy-hour event. Sonya and I were seated several chairs away from each other, which made it necessary for me to venture over to where she was to have a chance to speak with her. Once we were able to chat, I was immediately struck by the energy that she brought to our conversation. It may not be what you think. It was not gregarious. It was not intense. It was not with want or need. It was mindful.

While I have tried at different times in my life — with little success — to develop a formal meditation practice, I have at least been successful in my attempt to practice mindfulness. Mindfulness means being fully in the present and focusing on the other person, absorbed in the situation and on the task at hand. Mindfulness means letting go of the "monkey mind," which is the restless, unsettled, and unfocused mind.

It is this mindfulness that I immediately experienced with Sonya. When we met, she was focused on our conversation and on what I was saying. Sonya was really listening, and I felt it. I realized that while we were newly acquainted, and much of our talk was the type of surface conversation that you have when you first meet someone, it did not matter. Sonya is simply fully present, whether the conversation happens to be heavy or light. I realized in that moment that her mindfulness prompted my own mindfulness. I felt the power that comes from being truly heard.

I thought that perhaps this level of mindfulness came from Sonya's experience as an Olympic Trials athlete, or from her past career in finance. Or maybe she was just born with it.

During our 50/50 Friendship Flow Challenge date, I asked her if she had always possessed this asset, this gift for being present. I wondered: Was it is something that she has had to work to cultivate?

To my great relief, Sonya shared that her mindfulness comes from practice. It is something which is vitally important to her and therefore she has cultivated mindfulness as part of her everyday being.

For over a decade and a half, Sonya has worked as an executive coach. I can only imagine how incredibly beneficial it is to her clients to have a coach like her who consistently practices mindfulness — not only in her career, but also in her personal life. Because of Sonya, I certainly have learned that applying my practice of mindfulness not just to my professional life as a women's life coach, but also beyond that — to my personal and social life as well — has made all my relationships much more fulfilling.

The 50/50 Friendship Flow Challenge Lesson: The more you practice mindfulness, the easier it is to tune out the ramblings and ranting of the monkey mind.

The 50/50 Friendship Flow Challenge to Take Action: Be fully present. Let go of distractions.

Journal

Today's date is:

I can practice shutting down my monkey mind. My daily mindfulness practice is:

The greatest gift that you can give someone is your full attention.

"Empathy is a
contagious talent."
—Shari Leid

Chapter 38

Practice Attuned Awareness

Date 38 — July 23, 2019, Tuesday
JOEY Southcenter, Tukwila, Washington
Happy Hour
Girlfriend: Sarah

S arah is one of those friends who will make your face light up when you see her. You can feel it. She has a constant sparkle in her eyes that lets you know she is excited about the time she will be spending with you. She will talk to anyone as if they are a lifelong friend. She has a natural way about her that brings joy to any group she is in. If you walk into a room where Sarah is present, you will leave with more than just one story about what Sarah said that had you in stitches.

Sarah is funny. There are funny people, there are quick-witted people, and there is Sarah. I compare her to a virtuoso. While there are great musicians in the world, there are only a few virtuosos — those unique individuals who can pick out the nuances of a certain sound, a rhythm, the spirit of a musical number, without effort. They are so attuned to the music, they can hear details that even some of the best musicians do not. That is Sarah with her humor. She is so tuned in, so aware, that nothing slips by her. Even when people are expecting her quick wit, she can catch them off guard.

It is easy to see *attuned awareness* in Sarah's sense of humor. What is often overlooked is that her uniquely keen awareness springs from all aspects of her life. It is what makes her such a compassionate friend. Sarah is one of the most giving individuals I know. Everything from Sarah comes from the heart. As I try to practice mindfulness, I look beyond that to Sarah, and realize that being attuned to everyone and everything around you is a large piece of the practice of living mindfully.

While Sarah was born with the gift of attuned awareness, it is something that can be practiced by anyone. Walk outside and take a moment to notice your surroundings. Notice the individual colors, the sounds, the feeling of the wind. When you sit down with individuals and listen to them, notice the tone of their voice, their body language — tap into the feelings they are expressing. The practice of attuned awareness supports mindful living.

The 50/50 Friendship Flow Challenge Lesson: Being attuned to your surroundings will enrich the experiences that you have in your daily life and strengthen your relationships.

The 50/50 Friendship Flow Challenge to Take Action: Go outside and just stand still. Pay attention. Notice what each of your senses picks up when you are experiencing the world with attuned awareness.

Journal

Today's date is:

_____

Today while practicing attuned awareness, I noticed:

_____

_____

_____

_____

_____

_____

_____

_____

_____

_____

_____

_____

_____

_____

_____

The world is overflowing with amazing details; it is an absolutely
delightful place to be.

"A person acting in angry is
never persuasive."
—Shari Leid

Chapter 39

Celebrate the Uniqueness of
Each Relationship

Date 39 — July 28, 2019, Sunday
The Cottage, Bothell, Washington
Coffee
Girlfriend: Susie

Susie is about my age — a little younger, but not by much. She is Korean American, mother of three boys, and married to her high-school sweetheart. Because she and her husband met at such a young age, they have literally grown up together, supporting and learning from each other along the way.

When I sat down with Susie, I asked her if she knew why I wanted to meet with her as one of my 50/50 Friendship Flow Challenge dates this year. My reasons could have been many, including chatting about her amazing muscular legs that are often commented upon; her crazy amazing cooking and baking skills; or the fact that she has given me a glimpse of what it would have been like had I grown up in my Korean biological family, instead of being adopted. But it was none of that. I met with Susie because I have been so impressed by her consistent ability to celebrate and respect every one of her friendships. When Susie finds herself caught in the middle of friends in conflict, I have noticed that she is able to be there for both "sides," without losing either friend or getting caught up in the drama. Anyone who has been caught in the middle of friends in conflict will recognize that this is not an easy spot to be in.

I asked Susie how she is able to navigate through these complex relationships. Her immediate answer was, "We're all adults." Then she proceeded to elaborate. My takeaway from our conversation is:

(1) Be authentic and honest in each relationship.

(2) Do not hide your relationships.

(3) If asked, remind everyone that each relationship is unique.

(4) Finally, let your friends know that relationships are not competitions.

The 50/50 Friendship Flow Challenge Lesson: Relationships are not competitions. Each friendship has its value.

The 50/50 Friendship Flow Challenge to Take Action: Be honest and genuine in all your relationships.

Journal

Today's date is:

_____

I am blessed with unique and authentic relationships, and here's what I'll
do to make sure they don't compete against each other.

_____

_____

_____

_____

_____

_____

_____

_____

_____

_____

_____

_____

_____

_____

Each relationship is a unique bond that carries its own
depth and beauty.

"You don't have to be perfect. You don't have to do everything."
—Shari Leid

Chapter 40

Aim for 80 Percent

Date 40 — July 30, 2019, Tuesday
Ascend, Bellevue, Washington
Happy Hour
Girlfriend: Renee

Renee is in her 40s, a true boss babe. Monday through Friday, she can be found dressed in beautiful fashion-forward career attire. On the weekends, she may be seen with a ponytail and baseball cap, attending an event with her daughters.

I explained to Renee that I wanted to meet with her as one of my 50/50 Friendship Flow Challenge dates because she always surprises me. She appears so laid back that you would not notice what a big deal she is until you, like me, start attending events around town and notice that you see her name everywhere. For example, I attended a *425 Magazine* event — *425 Magazine* is a regional business, arts, and entertainment magazine — and learned there that the magazine had named Renee CPA of the Year. Then there were various other non-profit events in the Seattle area that I happened to attend, only to find that Renee was volunteering — on the board, on a committee, or in some significant way — giving back and supporting our local community.

I had to find out how she does all of it. How does she remain incredibly busy, yet always seem so happy? I checked in with her: "You always seem so happy. You are happy; right?" She confirmed my observation. She is genuinely happy.

I asked Renee to share her secret, because I believe everyone's ultimate goal in life is not pleasure, money, or status; it's to find happiness. I also believe that happiness is found when you can find a balance of spiritual, physical, intellectual, relational, and emotional elements in your life. So, I wanted to know how this killing-it career woman, mom of two teenagers, friend to all, and superstar community volunteer balances everything to such a degree that she is not only successful but also happy.

Renee's answer surprised me, and it made me laugh. I am so thankful for the fact that happiness is an attainable place to be. She responded, "I'm an 80-percenter." She went on to explain how she always performs at a very high level; and, at one of her employment reviews years ago, the supervising partner told her how much she added to the firm and how she was worth much more than they were paying her. The partner made it a point to let her know that the firm realized, recognized, and acknowledged her value. But then he shocked her. He said, "But, Renee, you're an 80-percenter." She had no idea what he meant. Was that good? Was it bad? What it came down to is that while she came through 100 percent on everything (so her firm always knew that she would complete whatever needed to be completed), it was the last 20 percent of the project that she would save for the last minute. Her supervising partner explained to her that while she gets everything done, that last 20 percent needed to be delegated — earlier rather than later — to prevent people around her from becoming unnecessarily stressed. As a great supervising partner, he emphasized that it is okay to be an 80-percenter; just own it, and always delegate that other 20 percent.

I hope I am doing Renee's message justice, because it really resonates with me. I immediately thought of how often we receive the message that we must always give 100 percent, if not 110 percent. No wonder we are overly stressed and not happy as a society. It is impossible to give 100 percent in every single endeavor, and for sure it is physically impossible to give 110 percent in anything.

The 50/50 Friendship Flow Challenge Lesson: Be an 80-percenter: Find life balance, and delegate that 20 percent whenever you can. Balance is where happiness lies.

The 50/50 Friendship Flow Challenge to Take Action: Decide today to delegate 20 percent of one of your current projects.

Journal

Today's date is:

_____

I am delegating the following 20 percent of today's to-do list:

_____

_____

_____

_____

_____

_____

_____

_____

_____

_____

_____

_____

_____

_____

Happiness is the ultimate goal. Life balance is the key.

"Happiness is impossible
without optimism."

—Shari Leid

Chapter 41

Practice Daily Meditation

Date 41 — August 3, 2019, Saturday
Pressed Juicery, Bellevue, Washington
Morning Juice
Girlfriend: Yolanda

Yolanda and I met several years ago when one of our mutual friends invited her to a party at my home. We have gotten together in groups, we have double-dated, and we have run into each other at the gym on several occasions; but the opportunities to get together one on one to really talk have been few and far between. I was definitely looking forward to our 50/50 Friendship Flow Challenge date — a rare chance to begin my Saturday morning with Yolanda.

When I picture Yolanda, I think of a friend who feels what those around her feel. I have a sense that she feels others' emotions more intensely than many of us. Believing this to be true, it was important for me to find out during our date how she is able to maintain self-care, while avoiding getting caught up in others' emotions without feeling drained. I can only imagine what a weight it must be to have such an acute sense of connection to so many people around her.

Without hesitation, Yolanda described her practice of meditation. She sets daily intentions as part of her meditation practice. She graciously shared personal examples of times when her intentions during meditation were manifested into reality. I was instantly struck by how sincere she is in her practice, and how heartfelt her belief is in the power of meditation for overall wellbeing. She strongly believes in the power of meditation to effectively cultivate the environment that she seeks.

Yolanda teaches me the power of quiet, stillness, and intention to manifest one's desires through a meditation practice. I left Yolanda feeling inspired. After our time together, I made a commitment to invest in my own meditation practice. I am not quite sure yet what form it will take, but I know it's time to incorporate meditation as part of my life journey.

The 50/50 Friendship Flow Challenge Lesson: To manifest your desires, there is great power in meditation.

The 50/50 Friendship Flow Challenge to Take Action: Practice setting your intentions with daily meditation. If you are new to meditation, start with three minutes today; do three minutes each day for awhile; then build from there.

Journal

Today's date is:

_____

Today I will start my new meditation practice. Each day this week, during my daily meditation, I will set the following intentions which will manifest into my reality:

_____

_____

_____

_____

_____

_____

_____

_____

_____

_____

_____

Be quiet. Be still. Meditate.

Chapter 42

Teach and Guide Your Children

Date 42 — August 6, 2019, Tuesday
Mercato Stellina Pizzaria, Bellevue, Washington
Dinner
Date: Alexis

I thought about whether or not I should ask my daughter to be one of my 50 dates. Did it make a difference that she is my daughter and not one of my girlfriends? She is 19 years old now — a young woman — and our relationship is evolving, with the many traits and values of a strong female friendship. She has actually taught me more about life and about myself than any other female influence in my life, and because of that, she is one of my 50/50 Friendship Flow Challenge dates — an incredibly special one.

I was thrilled that Alexis agreed to be one of my 50 dates. First, it was important to me that I share with her what she has taught me. I did not want to do this just in passing; I needed her to hear how she is not only my daughter but also one of my greatest teachers. I shared with her that among many things, she has taught me that often when I became upset with her over a situation she was in, it was because I was comparing my own journey to what I thought her life should look like, rather than honoring *her* journey. I admitted that there were times when I acted like I had a right to direct her life, as if I owned her.

I asked her if it is hard to have a mom who is very social. She told me something incredibly wise. She said sometimes indeed it was difficult, and sometimes she felt jealous; but then she figured out that it was stupid to be jealous, because we are two different people — and I could never be her and she could never be me. This is something she could see early in life and discovered all on her own: Let go of comparison with or jealousy of other people, and just accept that we are all different. Furthermore, she observed, since each of us is unique, it makes no sense to compare ourselves to one another.

Alexis explained how the obstacles she has faced — whether learning differences or social challenges — have all made her stronger. She recognizes that she is a better person because of what she has experienced. I agree with her completely. She has not only been transformed after going through some hard times, but she has done so with the acknowledgement that these difficulties have pushed her forward. She understands that challenges have served her growth.

I continue to learn from Alexis. And the lesson that stands out to me the most — as our date occurred three weeks away from her leaving the nest for college — is that my kids' journeys are not mine; they are their own. And, what is best for them in my mind may be entirely different from what is truly right for them.

This young woman is learning to live without judgment and competition. She easily celebrates all the differences that make each of us so uniquely interesting and wonderful. I am incredibly blessed to be Alexis' mom. And I feel strongly that the fact that both of us were orphaned in different countries 30 years apart, and that we're here together now, means that there must have been a grand plan out there: We were always meant to be mother and daughter — a family.

The 50/50 Friendship Flow Challenge Lesson: My children's journeys are theirs to take, not mine. I do not own them.

The 50/50 Friendship Flow Challenge to Take Action: Be a teacher and a guide for your children (or for any young people you love) — remembering that each of us has a unique path to travel in life.

Journal

Today's date is:

I will not judge nor do I own my children (or any of the young people I love).
I am here to teach and guide, which means that I will do the following:

We are all on a distinctive life journey, each of which
is uniquely our own.

"Talk to your children in the voice you want them to remember you by."

—Shari Leid

Chapter 43

Live Out Loud

L inda has dark hair, which she wears in a smart, edgy cut. She enjoys fashion, so she is frequently dressed up at various events around town, supporting causes she believes in — most often related to the tech industry, the arts, and uplifting women. Today was one of the first times I saw Linda dressed down, donning a casual look for our planned day of sailing after our 50/50 Friendship Flow Challenge date.

I always know what I want to share with each friend when I'm getting ready for our date because I think about the person quite a bit leading up to our time together. It is important to me that what I say comes from my heart and is communicated well. The first thing that came to my mind when I thought of Linda is that she lives out loud. Because I wanted to be accurate in my description of what I wished to share, I did a quick check with the *Urban Dictionary* to make sure there was not some other meaning associated with the term I chose to describe her. In this case, the definition could not have been more spot-on to what I'd hoped to convey. In fact, I could not say it better myself.

> The *Urban Dictionary* describes "living out loud" as:
> Being yourself — genuine, open, and trustworthy — with sass, spice, and flare. Living on purpose, loving others and yourself, living passionately for your values, no matter what. Letting others see your light shine, and not being scared to be different or worrying about others' opinions of you. Living a life you're excited about, with purpose on your terms. Inspiring others to do the same.

Linda is constantly connecting people. Linda seems to flow from meetings to events throughout the day, much related to her PR marketing media firm, and in equal parts to support her friends and the local arts. The underlying theme to everything Linda does is *support*. Despite her full schedule, if she is able to make it to a colleague's or friend's event — whether it be a business event or a social event — she will make it a point to be there to support, invite, and share. She doesn't just move forward herself; she's always taking others forward with her. Linda is always seeking an opportunity for someone else, not just a win for herself.

One of Linda's distinguished talents is her ability to create and orchestrate an event to bring a community together. She is able to lead effectively because she is not afraid to live out loud. She does not hesitate to invite people in to enjoy extraordinary experiences — educational, political, humanitarian, or social.

Linda reminds me that life is not to be wasted; every single day is an opportunity to live out loud.

The 50/50 Friendship Flow Challenge Lesson: When you're living with drive and verve, you're living life to the fullest.

The 50/50 Friendship Challenge to Take Action: Choose to live with purpose and panache: Live out loud today!

Journal

Today's date is:

Today here's how I will live out loud:

Life is meant to be experienced to the fullest.

"Do not be silenced."

—Shari Leid

Chapter 44

Let Go of Limiting Beliefs

Date 44 — August 22, 2019, Thursday
Salty's on Alki, Seattle, Washington
Lunch
Girlfriend: Rosa

Rosa is a Latina woman, in her mid-60s, with the energy of a much younger woman. When she smiles, she smiles with her entire face; her eyes light up and you immediately feel welcome in her presence. I am so honored to be able to call Rosa my friend. She is a trailblazer. She was the first woman of color to be a United States Marshall, she is a former police officer, and the list goes on.

I was excited to sit down with Rosa for our 50/50 Friendship Flow Challenge date to learn what inside her allowed her to enter these predominately white male careers and believe that she belonged there. I wanted to learn how to raise my daughter so that she will believe, too, that she can keep following her dreams.

Rosa shared with me that she has always believed she can do and be anything. She gave her mother much credit for raising her to believe in herself. When Rosa saw a place where faces did not look like hers, instead of shrinking back and making herself smaller (as many of us do), she made herself louder and larger, knowing she had her own voice.

Not only did Rosa have an amazing career in law enforcement, serving local communities and our country, she has continued to be an advocate for women rising through the ranks in all careers.

Rosa shared a vivid memory with me of her mom. One day in the midst of making tamales, her mom received a telephone call from a very high-level politician. Her mom's response was to tell him that she was busy, so he should call back in two hours. Rosa's mom taught her that your title, your skin color, or your gender do not matter. We all put our pants on one leg at a time.

She also shared an important lesson about rising through the ranks — whether it be in one's career or climbing the social ladder. It is always important to remember to be kind to the people you pass on the way up, because those same people will be the ones you see again when you're on your way down.

Tonight, I am going to remind my kids to remember that everyone puts their pants on one leg at a time. Each of us is just as valuable as the next. Just because your face is not a common type seen in a particular field, at a social event, or in a neighborhood, it does not mean that you do not belong. On the contrary, it means that those people really need you to be there.

The 50/50 Friendship Flow Challenge Lesson: You can do and be anything. Keep following your dreams.

The 50/50 Friendship Flow Challenge to Take Action: It's time to let go of limiting beliefs.

Journal

Today's date is:

_____

Today, I will follow my dreams. I will let go of the following limiting beliefs
that have been standing in my way:

_____

_____

_____

_____

_____

_____

_____

_____

_____

_____

_____

_____

_____

I belong. I have my own voice, and there are no limits to
what I can be and what I can do.

"Start a new story."

—Shari Leid

Chapter 45

Try Action and Reflection, Reflection and Action

Date 45 — August 26, 2019, Monday
Cactus on Alki, Seattle, Washington
Happy Hour
Girlfriend: Amber

O ther than my daughter, Amber is the youngest of my 50/50 Friendship Flow Challenge dates. Amber is in her late 20s, she's recently married, and she carries herself with the beauty and grace that reminds me of a glamorous Hollywood starlet from the 1920s.

I was really looking forward to our 50/50 Friendship Flow Challenge date. Amber and I met just a little shy of a year ago, embarking on a year-long journey together as we built and refined our professional skills. Both of us passionate about our work as life and career coaches, we were partnered together as part of our advanced skills–building training. I absolutely loved working one on one with Amber.

Amber reminds me so much of myself at her age — but she is actually ahead of where I was, because she really seems to know who she is much clearer than I did at 29. Of course I have the benefit of my age now — turning 50 in December 2019 — to be able to hang out my office shingle just about anywhere, and I will be trusted as having experience simply because of my age. Amber, on the other hand, often has to overcome the presumptions that come with being a young woman working in a profession where most people are 10–20 years her senior.

Getting to know Amber over the course of the past year, I was able to observe how much she brings to the table. She contributed so much insight and wisdom to every meeting. I think the easy answer to why she was able to do this would be that she is an "old soul." That is the easy catch-all answer, but it does not give her the credit for what she has somehow already mastered.

The traditional view is that with every birthday we have, we grow. While this may be true for children, this is not always the case once we reach adulthood. In adulthood, it is not the rotation around the sun that brings growth. Rather, it is the continuous cycle of action and reflection. We grow when we are able to deliberately combine the two. And that is what Amber does.

Amber reflects and acts, then acts and reflects. In my experience, the norm is that people tend to do one or the other. Either people *act*, and then if things go wrong (or even right) they are afraid to *reflect* honestly upon their role, their intent, or the effect they had on others; or, they *reflect* for so long, that they reach a point where they do not *act*, because they are too afraid of failing — thus experiencing "paralysis by analysis." Amber has already learned how to avoid these traps.

Being 20 years' Amber's senior, I felt it was my responsibility to share what I see in her. I told her that I have observed her exceptional ability to work with and lead people twice her chronological age because of her constant growth, which comes from engaging in a consistent cycle of action and reflection — an essential practice that has given her so much more wisdom than the mere years on the calendar would indicate.

The 50/50 Friendship Flow Challenge Lesson: Action and reflection, reflection and action — not trips around the sun — are what bring on true personal growth and change.

The 50/50 Friendship Flow Challenge to Take Action: Reflect upon your role in an action you have taken.

Journal

Today's date is:

For my personal growth, I choose to embark on a continual practice of action
and reflection, and reflection and action. Today I will reflect upon the actions
I have taken. Later, I will act upon these reflections:

I am responsible for the actions I take.

"Don't waste today by reliving yesterday."

—Shari Leid

Chapter 46

Get Involved in Your Community

Date 46 — September 4, 2019, Wednesday

Woodblock, Redmond, Washington

Happy Hour

Girlfriend: Belinda

Belinda and I met at our kids' grade school. Our children were not in the same grades, and we only overlapped for two and a half years at the school; however, because of our school volunteer work, Belinda and I had the opportunity to spend time together in meetings and at events, where we became easy friends.

Over the years, I have been able to observe the way Belinda parents her children, the way she leads, and how she gets involved in her community. While running her own firm, focusing on strategical consulting and financial management for small businesses, she still finds the time to be highly involved with her kids' activities and schools, with her neighborhood, and with her alma mater. Belinda does not sit on the sidelines.

I have witnessed first-hand how her community involvement has impacted her children. She reminds me that to raise kids by example is far more effective than merely giving lip service. Her kids have studied abroad; they've been involved in many extracurricular activities; and they are comfortable in new situations with new groups of people. Belinda has raised children who don't sit on the sidelines.

Belinda is one of my 50/50 Friendship Flow Challenge dates because she shows me that it's important to lead by example. When it is often much easier to sit on the sidelines, I am reminded of Belinda, who always gets involved and makes the most of life's opportunities.

The 50/50 Friendship Flow Challenge Lesson: Do not sit on the sidelines of life.

The 50/50 Friendship Flow Challenge to Take Action: Take hold of every opportunity to get involved in your community.

Journal

Today's date is:

_____

Here's how I will stay involved in my community:

_____

_____

_____

_____

_____

_____

_____

_____

_____

_____

_____

_____

_____

_____

_____

Happiness is found when we participate in life, making strong communities.

Chapter 47

Let Go of the Fear of Judgment

Date 47 — September 5, 2019, Thursday
Hearth, Kirkland, Washington
Happy Hour
Girlfriend: Kate

Originally from Paris, France and most recently calling Washington State home, Kate is a mom to a handsome middle-school-aged son who constantly amazes her with his intellect, kindness, and athleticism. Kate has so many layers. She and I met about eight or nine years ago. Over the past several years I have watched Kate immerse herself in a string of different projects — fashion designer, stylist, high-fashion model, kickboxing fitness instructor, and yoga instructor.

Kate is always moving forward, and she is not afraid to change direction when a different path makes more sense. While many of us get stuck in looking at life as a place of *either/or*, Kate lives life inside the *and*. She recognizes the potential of living life to the fullest. Her philosophy is that you can be anything *and* everything you want to be.

We had such a great 50/50 Friendship Flow Challenge date. I asked her what her secret was. How was she able to incorporate so many facets into her life? She explained that she is able to be involved in so many different activities because she has been able to let go of the fear of judgment by others. This freedom has allowed her to veer off in a new direction whenever necessary. She allows herself to follow her passions. She is not held back because of worry over what others may think of her.

I love seeing how Kate's gentleness with herself has allowed her to experience life to the fullest. Her work, her talent, and her heart are all centered in helping women discover who they truly are on the inside, and then she helps to complement that individual spirit with physical exercise, nutrition, and fashion. The number of lives she continues to transform through her gifts are countless. In her work with women, she teaches them to express themselves without fear of judgment. I love surrounding myself with friends like Kate — women who have mastered the art of letting go of the fear of judgment so they can live life their way.

The 50/50 Friendship Flow Challenge Lesson: You can be anything and everything that you desire. You can live life your very own way.

The 50/50 Friendship Flow Challenge to Take Action: Consider all the things that make you who you are, and look at all the things that letting go of the fear of judgment from others will allow you to be.

Journal

Today's date is:

_____

I don't care what other people think of my choices. I celebrate the following qualities that make me who I am:

_____

_____

_____

_____

_____

_____

_____

_____

_____

_____

_____

_____

_____

I can do many things. Anything!

"Choose to make today your best day ever."

—Shari Leid

Chapter 48

Invite Friends into Your Home

Date 48 — September 10, 2019, Tuesday
Heritage Restaurant and Bar, Woodinville, Washington
Dinner
Girlfriend: Cindy

Cindy radiates love and beauty. She definitely turns heads when she walks into a room. She has an impeccable sense of style and she is friendly to everyone she meets. Of German and Mexican descent, she grew up in a number of places around the world before calling Washington State home. She and her husband created a blended family, and they're having the best time together now that their four adult children are all out of the house and successfully thriving on their own.

Cindy and I met nearly 14 years ago at a dinner party. We met through a mutual girlfriend who is still a special part of both our lives. It is fitting that Cindy and I met this way, because bringing people into her home, especially her girlfriends, is what Cindy does so consistently well.

I have met so many wonderful women through Cindy. She really has created a lifetime of amazing memories for me through gatherings at her house. Some of these get-togethers are large, and others are more intimate. It does not matter how many people are there; the warmth that she provides is consistent throughout. She has the ability to make everyone feel not just welcome, but incredibly special to be invited into her beautiful home. Each time I am invited over to Cindy's house, I am greeted with the same warm welcome from her, which sets the tone for the entire evening.

Cindy reminds me that to cultivate relationships, it is important to open my home to others, especially to share a meal. After experiencing the positive effects of Cindy's hospitality, instead of hosting only a yearly social gathering at my house, as I have done in the past, I'd like to try to host more often. I have learned from Cindy the exceptional warmth that comes from opening one's home to friends.

The 50/50 Friendship Flow Challenge Lesson: Your home is where your heart is. It's a gift to invite people in.

The 50/50 Friendship Flow Challenge to Take Action: Plan something special: Invite friends to gather at your home.

Journal

Today's date is:

_____

I will make a plan for an event to fill my home with friends:

_____

_____

_____

_____

_____

_____

_____

_____

_____

_____

_____

_____

_____

Home is where the heart is.

"You must do things that you
think you cannot do."
— Eleanor Roosevelt

Chapter 49

Embrace Your Many Purposes

Date 49 — September 11, 2019, Wednesday
The Cottage, Bothell, Washington
Brunch
Girlfriend: Bernadette

Bernadette is a beautiful Black American woman who is in her 60s but she has the energy of a woman in her 40s. She has the ability to talk to anyone, and she makes friends everywhere she goes. Her personality is infectious.

I am so honored to be a part of Bernadette's life. She is living her purposes. Yes, that is *purposes*, plural. And Bernadette taught me that.

Bernadette and I decided upon brunch for our 50/50 Friendship Flow Challenge date. I started out by commenting on how she is living her purpose, and without hesitation she corrected me, saying, "purposes." Bernadette reminded me that we can live many purposes simultaneously, and throughout our lives. We do not need to be confined to the idea that we are here on this Earth for only one purpose.

I find her point of view so freeing, because so often — especially when we get to the second half of life — we start to contemplate in earnest what our purpose is, what we have been put on this planet to do. Recognizing that we have the ability to live and pursue multiple avenues with the gifts we have been given — and that we do not have to be restricted to only one direction — makes life feel just that much more exciting.

Bernadette's life certainly is one that embodies a life of purposes. She was the first artist to be signed by Stevie Wonder's label, and she performed in Vegas — including opening the Motown Cafe, which drew in every celebrity you could imagine. Throughout Bernadette's career she has been drawn to teaching children. While she is a talented vocal coach, she is also an innovator. She created a spelling program that uses music to teach students to spell for the schools of Baltimore, Maryland. Most recently, she has created The Music Project for the Northshore School District in Washington State. Bernadette was the subject of an Emmy-winning documentary about her work with The Music Project, entitled *Bernadette's Touch*. And now, her work will soon be able to reach more kids and families with an app being developed by a leader in the software industry that will allow parents and families anywhere in the country to work with their children at home to help promote the child's language skills using the music program that Bernadette invented.

Children of all ages are naturally drawn to Bernadette. While we were at brunch together, I witnessed small children looking at her with awe. In each instance, Bernadette immediately took the time to recognize them. I believe little children have the natural ability to see a loving spirit, so I am not surprised that they are drawn to Bernadette. She is a tender, caring soul, and everything she does shows what "living a life of purposes" means.

The 50/50 Friendship Flow Challenge Lesson: You have been put here on this Earth for many purposes.

The 50/50 Friendship Flow Challenge to Take Action: Think about the many purposes that you have served, that you are currently serving, and that you will serve in the future.

Journal

Today's date is:

My past, current, and future purposes abound.

The world is a better place because of me.

"Leave everyone you come across happier, simply because they met you."

—Shari Leid

Chapter 50

Light Up a Room

Date 50 — September 17, 2019
Fern Thai on Main, Bellevue, Washington
Lunch
Girlfriend: Michele

Michele's positive energy is through the roof. From the first time I met Michele, I was impressed by her ability to brighten up a room. We all know people who can drain the energy *out* of a room — a co-worker, friend, or relative. When it comes to these energy-sucking types, we have to gear up beforehand in order to have enough energy ourselves to deal with them. But then there is Michele, the total opposite of that. She is one of the rare few who can light up any place she enters. She is one of those individuals who, if you are hosting a gathering, you become very excited about as soon as you find out that she's going to be there, because you know that it means everyone around her will have a better time. Michele's good energy is simply that strong.

I have been thinking about the type of energy people bring into a room for a little while now. In the past, I always thought that the ability to change the energy of a room either positively or negatively was a skill other people had, not something that I had the capacity to do. I guess I thought of myself more as someone who just follows the energy of the room and goes with the flow. This is no longer my belief. In fact, each one of us has the power to change the energy of a room, a group, or even the energy of another human being. I recognize now that I, too, can uplift the spirits of others, just like Michele does.

I really wanted to know precisely how to do this with the ease Michele possesses. During our 50/50 Friendship Flow Challenge date, I told her that I believe she must have possessed this ability to brighten up a room and increase the positive energy of those around her from day one. I needed to know where this superpower came from. She shared with me that her dad had the same type of energy that I see in her. When Michele's dad walked into a room, people instantly knew he was there, and they wanted to be around him. Michele also told me that it really comes from being comfortable with who you are — letting go of external and internal blocks that prevent you from being comfortable in your own skin.

She did not use these exact words, but what I heard her saying is that you have to let go of ego. Let go of the fear of judgment from others. And, as I was thinking about her advice while driving home from our lunch date, I found that I felt relaxed — and liberated. While I had already been focused on living with more intention regarding how I show up in life, the idea that I can simply be myself feels absolutely freeing. And what a perfect message to end with as the last of my 50/50 Friendship Flow Challenge dates comes to a close: *Just be you.*

The 50/50 Friendship Challenge Lesson: Just be you. You are enough!

The 50/50 Friendship Challenge to Take Action: Before you enter a social gathering or business meeting, notice and choose the energy that you will bring into the room.

Journal

Today's date is:

I can light up a room when I walk in, with the positive energy I choose to bring.

You have the power to increase the positive energy in any room you enter.

Epilogue

Thank you for taking this journey with me. I am excited to hear about your own experience as you embark on your 50/50 Friendship Flow Challenge. And, as you embark on the Challenge, please remember:

We attract people into our lives for a reason, whether it be for a moment, a weekend, a season, or a lifetime. We are teachers and students for one another. Every interaction is always an opportunity to grow, learn, and teach. As you reflect on the people in your life, take no one for granted. As you become more focused on the purpose of the relationships in your life, you will soon see that everyone who comes into your life has something very important to teach you as you go along life's journey.

When we realize our connection to everyone, we are no longer in competition. We no longer feel conflict, and we no longer feel alone. We live without the fear of judgment. We live with the ability to venture out onto a new path when needed, to have many purposes — to live our best authentic life.

Relationships are important for our overall wellness, happiness, and longevity. Nurture and appreciate all of the relationships you have been given in life. Enjoy your 50/50 Friendship Flow Challenge journey!

About the Author

S hari Leid was born in Seoul, Korea. At just a few weeks old, she was orphaned. After a year of living in both an orphanage and a foster home, she was adopted by an American family in November 1970. She currently resides in Woodinville, Washington with her husband and two very active English Labradors. Both of her children are in college, the first adopted from China, and the other born just eight months after she and her husband adopted. Two children in one year!

Shari is a former litigator, having graduated from law school in 1995. She currently operates An Imperfectly Perfect Life, LLC, a professional life coaching business serving women, helping guide them towards recognizing their power.

Shari's experience as an adoptee, and as mother to a neuro-difference adopted child has taught her patience, compassion, and resilience. She is a woman who has survived a catastrophic car accident, a double joint replacement, and breast cancer — all of which have given her a unique perspective on life's journey, allowing her to relate to each of her clients on a deep level as she provides encouraging support through their many challenges and helps them express their singular uniqueness.

All of Shari's life obstacles have brought her farther than she could have ever imagined. Her purpose in life — her passion — is to help other women find their own passion in order to achieve ultimate happiness...because happiness is really everyone's ultimate goal.

Contact Us

An Imperfectly Perfect Life
PO Box 592, Redmond, WA 98073
Tel. 206-225-7643
www.animperfectlyperfectlife.com

Made in the USA
Monee, IL
17 October 2021